Geelong & The Bellarine Peninsula – The Spirit of Place

Published
November 2004

Published by
Best Shot! Publications Pty Ltd ACN 100 252 926
2/16 Coronation St, Geelong West, Victoria 3218, Australia

ISBN 0-9756023-1-4

Cover: Robert Bole, Spring Creek, Torquay Back Beach
Back cover left: George Stawicki, Swan Bay
Back cover right: George Stawicki, Moorabool River
Inside cover: Robert Bole, Queenscliff

Printed in China by Twin Age Limited, Hong Kong, email: twinage@netvigator.com

Geelong & the Bellarine Peninsula

Richard Everist

The Spirit of Place

BestShot!

Best Shot! Publications: Ballarat, Bendigo, Croydon, Geelong, Flinders, Taradale

CONTENTS

INTRODUCTION

Geelong and the Bellarine Peninsular can puzzle. They are a mystery, a conundrum. Few cities in the world have a more beautiful location, but few people think of Geelong as a beautiful place. Few peninsulas in the world are as extraordinary, but few people think of the Bellarine Peninsula as extraordinary.

Geelong hugs the shores of a wide, shallow lagoon now known as Corio Bay, the western arm of Port Phillip Bay. Prior to the dredging of a shipping channel at Point Henry, at low tide it was virtually possible to walk the entire distance between the southern and northern shores. Prior to the arrival of European technology, the bay was a green and blue food bowl, rich in shell-fish, fish and water birds and a key part of a flourishing Aboriginal culture.

On its western side Geelong is circled by a ring of extinct volcanoes, and granite ridges. The most prominent and distinctive are the You Yangs – the blue silhouette of the You Yangs is Corio Bay's signature, a constant reference point from virtually any outlook in the region. There is a gentleness to the You Yang's low-lying symmetry but this is warped by an aura of strangeness and enormous age. They evoke a time when they sat in a sea of volcanic flows from the volcanoes at Anakie, Moriac and Duneed, on the eastern rim of Victoria's magnificent volcanic plains.

The northern shores of the Bellarine Peninsula look out across Corio Bay, and Port Phillip Bay. The views are full of water and sky and can turn swiftly from sheltered stillness to a wild maelstrom. Whatever happens in the sky is reflected and explosively magnified in the waters of the two bays.

Queenscliff is at the easternmost point of the peninsula, a grand Victorian-era town that stands surrounded by fortifications at the mouth of Port Phillip Bay. This is where 2000 sq kms of trapped water joins Bass Strait – through the Heads, which are just 3.5 km wide. The meeting of wind, wave, tide, pilot boats, and shipping creates the 'Rip', one of the most dramatic maritime scenes in the world – and one of the world's great dive sites.

The southern shores face Bass Straight and catch the full force of waves generated by the Roaring Forties in the Great Southern Ocean. White sand beaches and surf-wrapped headlands run the entire length of the coast – culminating with the legendary big waves at Bell's Beach.

Left: Joe Mortelliti, Spray Farm Lane
Top Above: Bruce Kirby, Ceres
Bottom Above: Robert Bole, Torquay

The hinterland of the Peninsula faces challenges posed by rapidly growing residential developments, but it is also increasingly valued for its environmental qualities, its history, golf courses, wineries and restaurants. Lake Connewarre, with its salt marshes and mangroves, is part of a fascinating wetland system that along with Swan Bay and the Lonsdale Lakes has been recognised as a flora and fauna habitat of international significance – especially for water birds.

The history of the City of Geelong is the history of European settlement in Victoria, and it bears the embellishments – and scars – from four economic phases.

The first boom in the 1850s was thanks to the greatest alluvial gold rush the world has ever seen, when Geelong was a major gateway to the western goldfields.

Then followed a long period where Geelong funnelled the Western District squatters' agricultural riches to the outside world, built a string of world-famous woollen mills along the banks of the Barwon River, and constructed massive wool stores overlooking the port.

From the 1920's and particularly after WWII, Geelong developed as a major industrial centre. Corio Bay was gradually surrounded by monolithic, multi-national industries: petrochemicals, cars, agricultural equipment and aluminium.

Today, a fourth phase is unfolding. Geelong is still a manufacturing centre, but it is increasingly defined by tourism, education, surf, scientific research, a community of artists, and thriving service industries. Driving this is a fresh appreciation that a regional city (not too big, not too small), set on a beautiful bay, less than an hour from a very large metropolis, and less than 20 minutes to great beaches - is a great place to be.

Left: George Stawicki, Barwon Heads
Top Above: Artist Photographer, Corio Bay
Bottom Above: Artist Photographer, Barwon River

GEELONG & THE BELLARINE PENINSULA

Left: Barry Feldman, Clifton Springs Sunset

HISTORY

GEOLOGY

The first Europeans gave no credence to cataclysmic stories of fiery mountains, and fertile plains engulfed in water that were told to them by the Aboriginal occupiers of the land. But western geology and archaeology have not only proven these stories to be true, but also proven the Wathaurong people were around to witness these events – in fact were around for 20,000 years before these events.

What is now Port Phillip and Corio Bays was once a fertile river plain, cut by the Yarra, Werribee and Little rivers. The rivers met at a deep gorge, which is now the mouth of the bay, and dropped to another lower series of plains that stretched into what is now Bass Strait. Indeed during an Ice Age 15,000 years ago there was a land bridge that stretched as far as Tasmania. At times the sea levels have been as much as 100 metres lower than they are today.

The last 10,000 years has seen a rapid rise in sea levels. First the land bridge with Tasmania was cut and eventually the sea flooded into the gorge and the shallow valley behind. The shipping buoys of today mark the river beds of yesterday. Although their land area shrank dramatically it is easy to imagine people adapting to the warmer weather and the new coastal riches. The flooded valley – now the bay - has a coastline length of 264 km and it covers 1930 square km. The deepest portion is only 24 metres deep and half the waters are shallower than eight metres.

The rocks underlying the region are greenstone (lepidolite) and granite formed 365 million years ago. These bedrocks show at Dog Rocks near

Batesford (the oldest rocks known in Victoria) and the You Yangs. The rest are buried under sedimentary rocks and volcanic basalt. Much of the sedimentary rock comes from sands and shells deposited when seas stretched over this region, in several places leaving behind vast limestone deposits.

The Western District Volcanic Plains extend from Melbourne to the South Australian border, and there are over four hundred known craters and vents. Volcanic flows began about 4.5 million years ago and ceased at Mount Gambier as recently as 5000 years ago. This region is currently dormant, but new eruptions are possible at any time. However, on average there has only been an eruption every 10,000 or so years, so on average the next eruption is not immediately due.

Left: George Stawicki, Dog Rocks
Above: George Stawicki, Dog Rocks

ABORIGINAL / KOORI

Archaeologists continue to make significant discoveries that impact on our understanding of the human settlement of Australia, but most agree Aboriginals arrived at least 60,000 years ago. In Victoria stone tools and bones in the Keilor area of the Maribyrnong valley date back 30,000 years, but it is likely that many ancient sites have been submerged under the rising sea.

In the Lake Condah region of Western Victoria the Gunditj Mara people constructed channels, weirs and stone fish-traps. These allowed the Gunditj Mara to create ideal conditions for harvesting eels and fish, which in turn resulted in high population densities and the construction of permanent stone huts clustered into villages.

The people of the Kulin nation (or, more properly, linguistic group) that surrounded Port Phillip and Westernport Bays also built sophisticated fish traps but there is no known evidence of stone huts. Among other finely crafted artifacts, the Kulin were notable for the elaborate possum-skin capes they made.

The Wathaurong sub-group of the Kulin occupied the area stretching south of Geelong towards Aireys Inlet, north to Ballarat, west to Beaufort and then south-east to the Werribee River, encompassing all of the land now described as Geelong and the Bellarine Peninsula. Within this area there were approximately 25 clans who each took responsibility for a particular ancestor site. About 2,000 archaeological sites have so far been found in the region. Three in particular, Buckley Falls, the You Yangs and the Bluff at Barwon Heads, were important sites on the seasonal food-gathering routes the clans followed.

Reliable population figures do not exist, but it likely there were never large numbers: perhaps 18,000 to 20,000 Kooris across Victoria, perhaps 700 Wathaurong. What is certain is that the moment Europeans arrived Wathaurong numbers began to decline rapidly.

In July 1836, Henry Batman, John Batman's s brother, and others in his party shot dead 10 Kooris (probably Wathaurong) at the Werribee River. From then on, violence was common. Large-scale resistance to the European invasion of Victoria was centred around Lake Condah, and it seems likely that at least some of the Wathaurong were caught up in what became known as the Eumeralla War (after the Eumeralla River).

Numerous skirmishes, mass poisonings and shootings continued for several decades. Disease probably had an even greater impact than violence and by 1853 the Wathaurong numbered 30 or 40 people. In 1856 John Stewart purchased two allotments bordering Armstrongs Creek (Toolim Beal, Stewarts Road, Mt Duneed) as a haven for 20 surviving Wathaurong – only twenty years earlier the free and proud owners of the entire region.

Left: The Barter, by Eugene von Guerard, courtesy Geelong Gallery
Above: Joe Mortelliti, You Yangs

Top: Joe Mortelliti, Corio Bay
Bottom: George Stawicki, Corio Bay
Right: Bruce Kirby, Cottage

EUROPEAN DISCOVERY & NAMES

No one has recorded the first European contact with the southern coast of Victoria. Many believe the Portuguese first came ashore in the 16th century, and the phantom 'Mahogany Wreck' at Port Fairy may indicate that some stayed for good. Geelong plays a part in this conjecture because in 1847 Governor La Trobe was shown a set of mysterious ancient keys that were found buried deeply in the ground at Limeburner's Point.

Certainly European whalers and sealers had plundered the south coast over the course of the 18th century – and diseases they introduced may have already decimated the Koori population prior to the arrival of permanent settlers.

From the turn of the 19th century the written record is more complete and certain. In February 1802 Lt John Murray, commander of the brig Lady Nelson, sailed into Port Phillip Bay, reaching Corio Bay on the 21st. He took possession of territory for the Queen on 8 March 1802, naming the bay Port King after Governor King. He was overruled by Governor King who renamed the bay Port Phillip after the first governor of New South Wales.

Hot on Murray's heels was the renowned explorer and navigator, Matthew Flinders, in his ship the Investigator. Believing he was the first to sight the huge expanse of water he charted the entire bay, landed on the Bellarine Peninsula (or Indented Head, as he called it), had several friendly meetings with the local Wathaurong and climbed the You Yangs.

'The country surrounding Port Phillip has a pleasing, and in many parts a fertile appearance; and the sides of some of the hills and several of the valleys, are fit for agricultural purposes. It is in great measure a grassy country, and capable of supporting much cattle, though better calculated for sheep ... '
- Matthew Flinders in Terra Australis [1 May 1802]

On 24 December 1824, the explorers Hume and Hovell arrived at Corio and noted the area was suitable for settlement. When they approached the local Wathaurong for the name of the region they were told 'Jillong' referred to the bay, and 'Corayo' referred to the land. Despite this, the early European settlers managed to confuse the two, calling the land Geelong, and the bay Corio. For many years it was commonly believed that Geelong meant white sea bird and Corio meant a small marsupial. Recent linguistic research has confirmed that 'Djilang' means the bay, and 'Kohria' means the land around the bay.

WILLIAM BUCKLEY

In October 1803 there was a short-lived attempt to establish a settlement on the eastern side of the Heads at Point Nepean – possibly in response to the presence of several French ships that were loitering in the region. Lieutenant-Colonel David Collins led a party of 50 settlers and convicts, but they failed to find adequate fresh water and returned to Sydney in December.

Buckley was a man of imposing physical presence, at least 6 feet 5 inches (nearly two metres) tall, and heavily tattooed. According to legend, he found a spear that had been left on a Wathaurong grave, and when the Wathaurong saw a giant white man holding a dead man's spear they believed he was a Wathaurong warrior reincarnated.

They left behind the first permanent European resident of Victoria, an amazing man, William Buckley. Born in England around 1780, Buckley was sentenced to life imprisonment. He managed to escape from the Point Nepean camp and to either walk around the bay to the Bellarine Peninsula, or to swim across the Rip. In any event he spent the next 32 years living – from all accounts, happily – with the Wathaurong.

In July 1835 he made what must have been an agonising decision to walk into John Batman's camp at Indented Head. The authorities recognised his potential value as a translator and he was given a pardon. Contemporary accounts depict a man caught in a chasm between two irreconcilable cultures. Several times Wathaurong sought his help, and there were also accounts of tearful meetings with his former companions. In 1837 the tension must have become unbearable because Buckley sailed for Hobart. He died in 1856, by which time authorities were only able to count 20 Wathaurong survivors from the group of 700 or so who had welcomed him.

Much of what we know about the Wathaurong way of life is thanks to Buckley's memoirs, but there was and is doubt as to how reliable some of the recorded observations are. Nonetheless, his was an extraordinary story, and the account of his life and adventures was published in 1852:

'....the tribes are divided into families: or rather, I should say, composed of them – each tribe comprising from twenty to sixty of them. They acknowledge no chief as being superior to the rest; but, he who is most skillful and useful to the general community is looked upon with the greatest esteem, and is considered to be entitled to more wives than any of the others.

...they used to take me out on calm evenings to teach me how to spear salmon, bream etc. Their manner is to get some dry sticks, cut them into lengths of ten or twelve feet, tie several of these together into a kind of faggot and to light the end. With this torch blazing in one hand and a spear in the other hand, they go into the water, and fish crowd around and are easily speared...'

Left: George Stawicki, Buckley Falls
Above: Bruce Kirby, Buckley Falls

Top: Barry Feldman, Bellbrae
Bottom: Bruce Kirby, You Yangs
Right: Joe Mortelliti, Corio Bay

BATMAN'S GEELONG DEED

In 1835, John Batman, an adventurous entrepreneur, was engaged to represent a group of ambitious sheep graziers (the Port Phillip Association) who were running out of room in Van Dieman's Land (Tasmania). He was briefed to explore and purchase land around Port Phillip. From his camp on Indented Head he took a route similar to that of Flinders 33 years earlier. He crossed Corio Bay, climbed the You Yangs and gazed over thousands of acres of natural grassland and recorded 'I never saw anything to equal the land in my life'.

In June he sailed his boat Rebecca up the Maribyrnong River, not far from the site he was to choose for the town of Melbourne. Here he signed two 'treaties' with the Kulin people to 'purchase' 600,000 acres of land between what is now Melbourne and the Bellarine Peninsula on behalf of the Port Phillip Association.

The contract for territory around Melbourne was known as the Dutigalla Deed, and the other, for Indented Head (the Bellarine Peninsula), was known as the Geelong Deed. The Geelong Deed covered:

'All that Tract of Country situated and being in the Bay of Port Phillip, known by the name of Indented Head, but called by us Geelong, extending across from Geelong Harbour almost due South, for ten Miles, more or less, to the head of Port Phillip, taking in the whole Neck or Tract of Land, and containing about One Hundred Thousand Acres.'

According to the treaty documents the land was transferred to Batman in exchange for blankets, knives, looking glasses, tomahawks, scissors, handkerchiefs, shirts, flannel jackets and flour, plus a yearly tribute or rental payment. The traditional landowners also gave Batman two cloaks, and some stone axes, woomeras, boomerangs and other tools, and allegedly confirmed the sale by making marks in trees with their axes.

History does not say whether the Kulin received all the goods that were promised to them, and some might wonder what has happened to their yearly tribute or rental payments! It certainly seems highly unlikely the Kulin Batman found around the Maribyrnong River had any right to give away Wathaurong land. Interestingly, the treaty was never recognised by government authorities. Whatever its faults, it made an assumption that was unacceptable: the land was 'owned' by Kooris.

Top: Geelong from Mr. Hiatt's, Barrabool Hills, by William Duke, courtesy Geelong Gallery
Bottom: Bush Burial, by Fredrick McCubbin, courtesy Geelong Gallery

SETTLEMENT & THE BIRTH OF GEELONG

Right or wrong, members of the Port Phillip Association and other squatters soon began to arrive at Port Phillip, landing their sheep at Williamstown, Indented Head, and increasingly at Point Henry.

John Cowie and David Stead were the first, in March 1836, and occupied Bell Post Hill and the Moorabool Valley. They were followed by the Manifold brothers, James Strachan, George Russell, George Armytage, Thomas Austin, Hugh Murray, and many others. Some of these pioneers founded great pastoral empires that continue to exist today; certainly their bluestone mansions still exist, evidence of the great wealth these intrepid robber-barons wrung from the lands they seized from the Wathaurong and Gunditj Mara.

These were exciting times. David Fisher ran flocks over the site of Geelong and by March 1837 had built the first substantial Geelong house. About the same time Dr Alexander Thomson established his Kardinia estate at what is now known as Belmont.

Captain Foster Fyans, a Police Magistrate, arrived, and the town was surveyed and gazetted as a town on 10 October 1838. It took until 1842 before all the trees on surveyed streets were removed, but there were already 82 houses and 545 people! The first Geelong Customs House was built in 1838, as a modest moveable structure that was placed near the first pier (it is Victoria's oldest surviving building and can now be seen at the Geelong Botanic Gardens). In 1839 the first wool stores were opened by Champion and Strachan.

There was a church, hotel, store and wool store, and the steamer Aphrasia began a regular ferry service between Geelong and Melbourne. On 21 November 1840 the Geelong Advertiser was launched by its editor James Harrison with the clarion cry:

Bring forth the Press!
When first that mighty shout was heard.
Truth rose in radiant light ensphered.
The Nations to address.

Harrison, who was working for John Pascoe Fawkner, is now better known for his invention in 1856 of the first mechanical ice-making process.

Christ Church (Anglican) at the top of Moorabool St, designed by Edmund Blacket, the pre-eminent architect of the time (famous for his buildings at Sydney University) was built from 1843 to 1847 and is the state's oldest church in continuous use.

Top: Bruce Kirby, Corio Bay
Bottom: Bruce Kirby, Rippleside
Right: Artist Photographer, Geelong Railway Station

THE PIVOT

The most important limiting factor for Geelong's development was the sandbar between Point Henry and Point Lillias: only 1.8 metres deep at low tide it meant that all large ships were forced to load and unload at Point Henry. Despite this major problem Geelong remained competitive with Melbourne because of its easier access to the Western District and even to Ballarat (from Melbourne you are forced to climb the Great Dividing Range).

Despite the fact that Melbourne had been chosen as the state's administra-tive centre, Geelong still laid claim to being the commercial centre thanks to its exports of wool, tallow, sheep, skins and salted mutton. This competition fed an intense rivalry between the cities. Geelong's supporters liked to refer to Geelong as the Pivot, thanks to its central geographic position and its pre-eminent role in Port Phillip's trade and commerce.

In 1851, the Geelong Advertiser made the first announcement of the discovery of rich alluvial goldfields at Clunes near Ballarat and one of the world's greatest gold rushes commenced. By 1852, 90,000 people had arrived to try their luck, and Geelong was often their first port of call. Geelong's population dipped as people disappeared to the goldfields, but then grew rapidly – from 8000 in 1851 to 20,000 in 1854 – making it the fourth largest town in Australia.

Momentum did not last however: Geelong was quickly overtaken in size by Ballarat and Bendigo, and dubbed 'Sleepy Hollow' by Melburnians - who were not beyond issuing a false map purporting to show the shortest and quickest road to Ballarat was via Melbourne. Geelong's population did not reach 30,000 for another sixty years. In 1857 the railway to Williamstown was opened and by 1862 it was extended to Ballarat and Melbourne proper. This had the effect of siphoning trade and people to Melbourne and even though the sandbar at the mouth of the bay was dredged in 1861 Geelong's race with Melbourne was over. By the 1860s the heaviest traffic in Australia was through the central goldfields between Melbourne and Bendigo, and by the 1880s, Melbourne was christened 'Marvellous Melbourne' – one of the biggest, fastest-growing, most modern and brashly confident cities in the world.

Top: Artist Photographer, Cheetham Salt, Moolap
Bottom: Joe Mortelliti, Corio Bay
Right: Artist Photographer, Wool combing machine

SLEEPY HOLLOW

Although Geelong would never again challenge Melbourne's overall commercial and cultural dominance it did not stagnate. Many fine domestic, civic and commercial buildings were constructed from the mid-fifties, including:

- Customs House, a beautiful sandstone Georgian-style building; corner of Brougham and Moorabool Sts; built in 1856
- Town Hall, built in the Greek Revival style; corner Gheringhap and Little Malop Sts; built in 1855
- Telegraph Office, another Georgian-style sandstone building; next to the old GPO, Ryrie St; built in 1858
- Merchiston Hall, a grand home built for James Cowie; 2a Garden St; built in 1856
- Geelong Gaol, built in 1852; open to the public
- The Hermitage, a grand sandstone home built for George Armytage; Pakington St; built in 1859
- Barwon Grange, a beautiful home built for Jonathon Parker O'Brien; Fernleigh St , Off Fyans St West; built in 1856; National Trust property open to the public
- The Heights, a prefabricated home set in grand gardens built for Charles Ibbotson; 140 Aphrasia St; built in 1855; National Trust property; open to the public.
- Matthew Flinders Girls High School, Little Ryrie St, old building built in 1856
- Geelong College, Talbot St, old building built in 1871

At the same time Geelong's industrial foundation – which was firmly based on the sheep and wheat of the Western District - was broadened with Donaghy's Rope Works on Pakington St (now mooted for retail development). Most importantly, however, in 1868 in response to a prize offered by the Victorian Government, Geelong investors built the first woollen mill in the state on Barwon Terrace, east of Landy Athletics Field: the Victorian Woollen & Cloth Manufacturing Company.

Over the coming decades wool scouring plants and textile factories lined the Barwon River, and Geelong's woollen products, and brands like Excelsior and Physician Blankets, became world-famous. Geelong entrepreneurs and families, among them the Hirsts, Grays, Shannons, Redpaths, and Collins, built huge mills that employed hundreds of people and woolbrokers (Dennys, Lascelles and Strachans) built their woolstores by the bay.

In 1875 the Barwon Woollen Mill was built next to the Victorian Woollen & Cloth Manufacturing Company Mill. Godfrey Hirst, a weaver, and Charles Shannon, a wool broker, purchased both mills in the 1890s renaming them Excelsior One and Two. These mills are still in use and continue to produce carpets under the Godfrey Hirst name. Some beautiful 19th century brick industrial buildings survive.

Geelong's iconic Fyansford cement works were opened in 1889 to exploit a vast limestone deposit at Batesford. They operated until late 2000 and the tallest chimney stacks in Australia (over 100 metres high, built in the 1960s) were demolished in 2004. Cheetham Salt, with its extensive evaporation ponds near Point Henry, began production of salt in 1894.

Top: Artist Photographer, Kardinia Park
Bottom: Artist Photographer, Kardinia Park

FOOTY

The history of Geelong is inextricably linked to the history of Australian Rules Football. Four men are credited with first codifying the rules. Tom Wills, his cousin Henry Harrison, WJ Hammersley and JB Thompson drew up 10 rules at the Parade Hotel, Wellington Pde, on 17 May 1859, making Australian Rules Football the oldest officially codified football game in the world.

There is growing consensus that these men drew initially on at least three sources: the informal games played by convicts and immigrants, rugby, and a Koori game, known as marngrook which was played by the Gunditj Mara of the Western District. It is also clear that Gaelic football has had a long term impact on the development of the game, but Gaelic football was not codified until 1884.

Harrison's family had a property near Moyston and Wills' family also had a property in the Western District. Harrison and Wills were both descended from emancipated convicts who were forced to fight bitterly for their rights within the colony and who were strongly pro-Australian. A unique Australian game, free of overt British influence would have appealed to them; it is also highly likely that both men would have at the very least seen, if not played, marngrook, which was described in 1841:

'The men and boys joyfully assemble when this game is to be played. One makes a ball of possum skin, somewhat elastic, but firm and strong. The players of this game do not throw the ball as a white man might do, but drop it and at the same time kicks it with his foot. The tallest men have the best chances in this game. Some of them will leap as high as five feet from the ground to catch the ball. The person who secures the ball kicks it. This continues for hours and the natives never seem to tire of the exercise.'

In 1849 Wills, who was a natural sportsman, was sent to Rugby School in England where he played the forerunner to rugby; he also played English County Cricket. On his return to Australia in 1856 he joined the Melbourne Cricket Club and regularly played at the Melbourne Cricket Ground (itself on an important Koori meeting site).

Top: Artist Photographer, Kardinia Park
Bottom: Bruce Kirby, Kardinia Park
Right: Artist Photographer, Kardinia Park

THE BLACK CATS

In July 1858 the first somewhat disorganized games football games were played between Melbourne Grammar School, Scotch College and a group of men calling themselves St Kilda. The matches went for days, and a lack of rules led to fights. As co-umpire of the Melbourne Grammar versus Scotch College match Tom Wills would have been acutely aware of the problem.

Three days before the rules were codified at the Melbourne pub in May 1859, the same group of four men had established the Melbourne Football Club. Tom Wills was also involved when the code's second club – the Geelong Football Club – was formed on the 18th July of the same year. Tom went on to play with a number of teams, but he and his brothers (who also played for Geelong) ended up with a clear allegiance to Geelong. Tom captained Geelong for six years from 1864 to 1869.

Henry Harrison was closely involved with the Melbourne and Richmond teams, but when he was transferred to the Geelong Customs House he also captained Geelong for a season. In 1869 he led Melbourne against a Victorian Police Force team in the first football game that was allowed to be played on the MCG.

Geelong was originally known as the Seagulls, but from the 1870s the team was known as the Pivotonians – based on Geelong's importance as the commercial pivot for the Western District and Port Phillip Bay. Geelong became the Black Cats in 1923 after a poor start to the season, and a cartoonist's suggestion that the team needed a black cat for luck.

The most important recognition that can be awarded to an Australian Rules player is the Brownlow Medal, which is awarded by umpires' votes for the season's best and fairest player. The Brownlow is named after Charles Brownlow who was an outstanding player, coach and administrator, closely associated with the Geelong Football Club for 40 years.

Brownlow was one of the best players in two Geelong premiership teams (1881 and 1882), captain of the premiership team in 1883 and coach of the premiership team in 1886. He went on to become an outstanding administrator, helping to establish the VFL when it broke away from the VFA. He was secretary of the Geelong club from 1888 to 1923 and VFL President in 1918-19. He died in 1924, and the first Brownlow Medal was appropriately awarded that same year to Geelong's number 20: Edward 'Cargie' Greeves.

Top: Bruce Kirby, Corio Bay
Bottom: Bruce Kirby, Wreck of the Ozone, Indented Head
Right: Artist Photographer, Corio Bay

STEAMERS

Although the importance of the role played by coastal steamers declined with the completion of the Melbourne railway in 1862 and the Queenscliff branch in 1879, a number of greatly-loved steamers continued to ply the waters of Port Phillip Bay up to 1942. They transported millions of passengers between Melbourne and Geelong and carried millions of holiday makers to Mornington, Sorrento, Queenscliff, Portarlington – and Point Henry.

Until a channel was dredged through the sandbar between Point Henry and Point Lillias all ships over about 200 tonnes were forced to load and unload at Point Henry. To meet this need several jetties and a township, including hotels and warehouses, were built.

After the channel allowed shipping into the inner harbour Point Henry became a popular holiday destination, attracting tens of thousands of visitors who arrived by steamer to enjoy tea rooms, music, dancing, entertainment, pony rides, picnic areas, and a camera obscura. Today nothing of this resort remains, and the entire point is engulfed by the massive Alcoa smelter. Only the views across to the You Yangs remain unchanged.

A number of entrepreneurs and companies ran steamers that catered for day trips around the bay, work parties, group picnics and moonlight cruises. The Edina was the longest running of the steamers and operated between Melbourne and Geelong from 1890 to 1938. It was 52 metres long and known as the 'Wicked Old Lady' for its record of colliding with other ships and escaping damage herself.

In 1886 the specially commissioned, Glasgow-built, Ozone reached the bay. It was 79 metres long, with unusually large paddle wheels, 6.4 metres in diameter. It housed a dining room, bars, a ladies' salon, and new-fangled

electric lights. It was known as the 'Greyhound of the Bay', was capable of speeds of 20 knots and could make the trip between Geelong or Queenscliff to Melbourne in less than two hours.

In 1890 the Ozone was joined by the even larger and more powerful Hygeia; at one time the fastest paddle steamer in the world, it reached speeds of 22 knots in trials on Port Phillip. Ninety-one metres long, it was licensed to carry 1600 passengers in luxury – there was even a barber's shop on board. The Weerona was one step larger again and was one of the fastest and most luxurious paddle steamers ever built. It operated on the bay from 1910 to 1942, was 94 metres long and could carry 2000 passengers. There was a hairdressing salon on board – and a bookshop!

The Ozone is still a part of day-to-day life on the Bellarine Peninsula. In 1925 it was stripped and taken to Indented Head to be used as a breakwater and pier. The old girl refused to cooperate however; in bad weather she swung around until she was parallel to the shore - and firmly stuck. Part of her boilers and one of her paddle wheels can still be seen. The Greyhound of the Bay now provides a diving platform for kids and an artificial reef for a myriad of fish.

INDUSTRY, PROGRESS, DISASTER

If gold and wool had defined and driven Geelong in the past, after WW1 the future lay with industry. In the Roaring Twenties the Corio Distillery, the Cresco fertiliser plant, the Phosphate Co-operative Company all opened around the north shore of Corio Bay. Most importantly, in 1925 the Ford Motor Company began assembly of its famous Model T.

In response to these developments new suburbs were surveyed for North Geelong, Bell Park, Corio, Norlane and North Shore. The population reached around 40,000, and Geelong, regained its place as Victoria's second largest city.

Although the Great Depression hit Geelong hard, industrial development continued in the latter half of the 30s. Pilkington set up their glass factory in 1937, the International Harvester Works opened beside Ford at North Shore, and vast bulk-handling facilities for wheat were constructed.

The Shell Oil Refinery opened at Corio in 1954, and to complete the encirclement of the bay, the Alcoa Aluminium Refinery opened at Point Henry in 1963. Post war Geelong saw a flood of immigration, driven by the opportunities created by these and associated industries. Housing Commission suburbs sprang up at Norlane and Corio. By 1965, Geelong's population was over 100,000, and the port was the fourth busiest in the country.

From the mid-seventies through to the nineties, Geelong faced a number of challenges. Much of the industrial base built up over the preceding century faced competitive challenges from overseas, and the Australian economy in general faltered several times. One by one Geelong's woollen mills (with the notable exception of Godfrey Hirst) closed. Increased demands for efficiency meant the old wool stores at the northern end of the city centre, clustered around Cunningham Pier, were abandoned – some becoming completely derelict. Unemployment and social problems increased.

Although the Waurn Ponds campus of the Gordon Institute of Technology became the first campus for Deakin University in 1976, and the Australian Animal Health Laboratory was opened in 1981, this was not enough to offset the seemingly inexorable decline in traditional manufacturing. Textile and footwear manufacturers continued to close (although the surf-wear manufacturers in Torquay were booming) and International Harvester walked away from their huge tractor and agricultural machinery works at North Shore. The massive Jackson's Abattoir at Corio Quay was also abandoned.

Finally, in mid 1989, the giant financier, Farrow Corporation, which had grown from a small accountancy firm in Geelong to a national institution, still based in Geelong, collapsed. Overnight thousands of Geelong savers, investors and businesses had their Pyramid Building Society accounts frozen, and ultimately millions of dollars were lost. Geelong's fragile self confidence – never overly strong since the days of Sleepy Hollow – was shattered.

Left: Robert Bole, North Shore
Above: Artist Photographer, Ford Motor Company

GEELONG, QUEENSCLIFFE & THE PENINSULA

In 1993 a new City of Greater Geelong was created from the former municipalities of Geelong, Geelong West, Newtown & Chilwell, Corio, Bellarine and South Barwon. Only the historic Borough of Queenscliffe (the name of the borough, which includes Point Lonsdale, is spelt with an 'e') has survived as an independent entity.

This almost medieval patchwork came complete with strong community identification, and much clinking of mayoral chains. Geelong West's city hall was at the north end of Pakington St, Newtown & Chilwell's city hall was at the top of the Pakington St hill, Corio was based at Osborne House, the Shire of Bellarine was based in Drysdale, and the Shire of South Barwon (which included Torquay) was based on Colac Rd, Highton.

The town of Queenscliff was founded in 1853, and was first and foremost built for Government purposes. It provided postal, customs, health and telegraph services, lighthouse and signal services, military establishments, and the sea pilots (to help ships navigate the Rip). It also thrived as a tourist destination, serviced by the bay steamers, and the town is still defined by magnificent architecture from the 19th century.

Today the Borough of Queenscliffe is the smallest Borough in Victoria, covering 13 square kilometres, with an estimated population of 3,500. The borough was created on 12th May 1863, and it is the only borough in Victoria to retain an elected Council since its establishment.

Although the township of Queenscliff is located on the Bellarine Peninsula, it is virtually an island, only connected to Point Lonsdale by a slender sand-dune isthmus called The Narrows, which separates Port Phillip Bay from Swan Bay.

Along with the rest of the Bellarine Peninsula, after the decline of the bay steamers, Queenscliff dozed for much of second half of the 20th century. Perhaps it is thanks to this lack of development pressure that Queenscliff's architectural heritage has been saved. The last 15 years has seen a strong resurgence of interest from Melbournians (who now arrive by car). Smart coffee shops and galleries line Hesse St. The old pubs have been renovated and restored and fibro shacks have given way to much grander homes, owned by retirees, city-escapees, and Geelong commuters.

Left: Joe Mortelliti, Swan Bay to Queenscliff
Above: Artist Photographer, T&G Building, Geelong

NINGHAM PIER

RECOVERY

The latter half of the 1990s and particular the first years of the new century have seen a steady recovery in Geelong and across the region. In 1996 Deakin University engaged the local architectural firm McGlashan Everist to recycle one of the old wool stores as a new waterfront campus. This was the catalyst for a major redevelopment of the waterfront, and the city began to reorient itself towards Corio Bay.

In 2003 an upgrade of the Geelong – Melbourne Highway was completed, and in 2004 an upgrade of the rail link. As Melbourne grew larger and the inevitable problems of a major metropolis become an inescapable part of its fabric, Geelong and the Bellarine Peninsula, with a (relatively) laid-back lifestyle, high-quality (relatively) unstressed resources, and (relatively) cheap real estate, became ever more appealing. Population growth resumed, and parts of the Bellarine Peninsula were among the fastest growing suburbs in the country.

The region now has a significant number of Croatians, Dutch, Germans, Italians and New Zealanders as well as many other nationalities. Deakin University and the Gordon Institute bring an influx of students from around the world, but particularly from Asia. In total, including Torquay, the total population of the region exceeds 200,000.

Where once over 30% of the population was engaged in manufacturing, now the figure is 17%. Employment by industry figures show 17% engaged in retail trade, nearly 5% in accommodation, cafes and restaurants, 8% in education, 11% in health and community services. Tourism now plays a vital role, employing 6% of the work force, with visitor expenditure at around $500 million a year.

The towns of the Bellarine Peninsula have experienced a real estate and tourism boom, driven literally by the phenomenon first identified by, and now named after, Sea Change, the hit ABC comedy that was set in Barwon Heads. Torquay is no longer a modest holiday resort, but a smart beachside satellite town and home to a world-leading surf industry. And the wineries of the hinterland are building a reputation for excellence.

Today the Geelong waterfront is a vibrant and fascinating place – nothing like the idyllic lagoon of Wathaurong days – nothing like the 19th century port that was filled with the world's fastest sailing clippers – but it is still a beautiful bay (now surrounded by the Gothic towers of refineries and factories), and still a working harbour (now with huge bulk carriers). All this, plus restaurants and good coffee!

Left: Robert Bole, Cunningham Pier
Above: Artist Photographer, Waterfront Restaurants

Top: Bruce Kirby, Eastern Beach
Bottom: Bruce Kirby, Eastern Beach
Opposite left: George Stawicki, Queens Park
Opposite right: Bruce Kirby, Cunningham Pier

EVENTS & FESTIVALS

There are a huge variety of events around the year and across the peninsula; only a few are listed here. For a complete listing and up-to-date information contact the City of Greater Geelong (tel 5227 0270, www.geelongcity.vic.gov.au).

AUSTRALIAN INTERNATIONAL AIRSHOW - AVALON

Every two years the Australian International Airshow is held at Avalon, showcasing new aviation and aerospace technologies. It features the latest military heavy metal, including attack helicopters, heavy lift, combat and combat support aircraft, as well as a vast array of civilian and commercial aircraft. Hundreds of aircraft are displayed.

The main focus is on the future, but the past is not forgotten and there are also antique aircraft, vintage war birds, pioneers of the jet age, and classics from the 40s and 50s. Highly skilled aerobatic experts also perform.

When: Every 2 years - next event to be held 15-20 March 2005

Location: Avalon Airport, Geelong

Phone: (03) 5282 0500

Email: airshow@airshow.net.au

Web: www.airshow.net.au

RIP CURL PRO – BELLS BEACH

The Rip Curl Pro at Bells Beach has become an annual pilgrimage for surfers every Easter. It's the world's longest running professional surfing event, with a history of innovation and excess stretching back to 1961, when the first contest was held, and 1973, when Rip Curl first sponsored the event. It attracts massive crowds every Easter and holds a proud place in surfing folklore. The natural amphitheatre at Bells Beach makes for an atmosphere unmatched anywhere in the world.

When: Easter

Location: Bells Beach, but movable and can follow the surf to Johanna

Phone: (03) 5261 0000

Web: www.ripcurl.com/events

SKANDIA GEELONG WEEK

Skandia Geelong Week is now established as Australia's largest keel boat regatta. The event attracts over 400 yachts and 4,000 competitors. The sailing program is matched on land with fireworks, aerobatic displays, and live music performances and outdoor dining along the Geelong waterfront. The event was first held in 1844 and is claimed to be the oldest sporting event in Victoria. The annual Regatta is part of Victoria's maritime history and now attracts competitors and visitors from both within Australia and internationally.

When: Australia Day weekend, January 2005

Location: Geelong Waterfront

Phone: 5229 9101

Web: www.geelongweek.com.au

EVENTS & FESTIVALS

BARWON HEADS FESTIVAL OF THE SEA

A variety of competitions, including the famous duck race and market day. This is a very enjoyable community festival.

When: 15-20 March 2005

Location: Barwon Heads

GALA DAY FESTIVAL

Gala Day is, historically, Geelong's spring festival celebration. Gala Day includes a colourful street parade through the Geelong CBD as well as a range of family-orientated activities at Johnstone Park.

When: 5 November, 2004

Location: Geelong

GEELONG SPRING CARNIVAL

The most exclusive event on the Geelong thoroughbred racing calendar, the Geelong Cup is a popular annual event that draws people (and horses) from all over Victoria. Catch a glimpse of a potential Melbourne Cup winner, try your luck at punting or enter the fashion stakes.

When: October

Location: Geelong Racecourse

Phone: (03) 5229 4414

HEAD OF THE RIVER SCHOOLGIRLS REGATTA

The Head of the River Schoolgirls Regatta draws in excess of 25,000 people to the Geelong region over the weekend the event is staged. Geelong's Barwon River course is the home of elite school-level rowing, proving itself to be one of the best venues in the state for rowing regattas. The Head of Schoolgirls Regatta began in 1985 and has been held in Geelong since 1987.

When: March

Location: Barwon River

HIGHLAND GATHERING

A Highland Gathering has been held at Queens Park in Geelong every year for nearly 50 years. The Highland Gathering brings together people to celebrate a day of sport, music and culture. Look out for traditional Celtic festivities, foods and dancing and try your hand at caber or haggis tossing!

When: late March

Location: Queens Park, Geelong

Phone: (03) 5227 0254

Left: Bruce Kirby, Avalon Airfield

Left: Artist Photographer, Corio Bay
Right: Artist Photographer, Pakington St

EVENTS & FESTIVALS

NATIONAL CELTIC FESTIVAL

The festival, based in Portarlington, is now Australia's biggest and most comprehensive celebration of Celtic culture, and it attracts more people each year. The National Celtic Festival embraces the Celtic countries of Ireland, Scotland, Wales, Cornwall, the Isle of Man, Brittany, Asturias and Galicia. The program boasts a high standard of local, national and international Celtic entertainment including music, dance, film, performing arts, craft, food and literature. Be moved by one of the most intriguing civilisations on earth. Experience the Celtic culture through the power of the people and the spoken word. Be enchanted by the vibrancy of its arts and the mystery of its past. Connect with its people, enjoy their energy and humour.

When: June

Location: Portarlington, Bellarine Peninsula

Phone: (03) 5241 2499

Email: celtic@pipeline.com.au

Web: www.nationalcelticfestival.com

PAKO FESTA

Experience multi-cultural Geelong first hand. A popular, annual event on Geelong's event calendar, the Pako Festa brings together many ethnic cultures in a street party atmosphere. A section of Pakington Street in Geelong West is closed for dancing, music, performances and an assortment of culinary delights. Fun for all the family.

When: February

Location: Pakington Street, Geelong West

Phone: (03) 5221 6044

Email: www.pakofesta.com.au

TOAST TO THE COAST

Toast to the Coast showcases cool-climate regional wines, local cuisine and top chefs in action. It's held at Deakin University's Waterfront campus and is open to anyone who enjoys a great day out. The event includes entertainment, wine and food tastings, cooking demonstrations and wine appreciation sessions provided by the Geelong region's wineries, restaurants and local producers.

When: late October

Location: Deakin Waterfront Campus, Geelong

Phone: (03) 5227 0214

QUEENSCLIFF MUSIC FESTIVAL

The annual Queenscliff Music Festival is fast becoming a major event, featuring a wide variety of musical and performance art, including blues, folk, world, jazz and acoustic to name just some. The event draws high profile Australian artists and is has a fantastic atmosphere.

When: 26-28 November 2004

Location: Queenscliff

Phone: (03) 5248 4816

Web: www.qmf.net.au

WOODEN BOAT FESTIVAL OF GEELONG

This new festival will celebrate wooden boats of all sorts - with sailing events, displays and exhibitions.

When: 12-14 March 2005 (Labour Day Weekend)

Location: Royal Geelong Yacht Club

Top: Richard Everist, Drysdale Market
Bottom: Richard Everist, Point Lonsdale Market

MARKETS

Markets have become a popular weekend focal point, with the best offering high-quality produce (including organic fruit and vegetables), crafts (from extreme kitsch to high quality), art (from the sublime to the ridiculous), and food (from sausages in bread to paella). The Bellarine Peninsula markets all have attractive locations, and make great starting points for a picnic and an explore.

OCEAN GROVE

Every first Sunday, 9.00am to 1.00pm

POINT LONSDALE

Every second Sunday, 9.00am to 2.00pm

DRYSDALE

Every third Sunday, 9.30am to 1.30pm

PORTARLINGTON

Every last Sunday, 9.00am to 2.00pm

QUEENSCLIFF

Every last Sunday, 9.00am to 2.00pm

BARWON HEADS

Barwon Heads Community Hall - each Saturday, 9.00am to 1.00pm

BECKELY PARK

Each Saturday, 8.00am to 1.00pm

BELMONT

Belmont Common - each Sunday, 8.00am to 1.00pm

GEELONG

Geelong Showgrounds - each Sunday, 8.00am to 2.00pm

GEELONG FARMER S MARKET

Little Malop Street Geelong - every second Saturday (each month), 9.00am to 2.00pm

STEAMPACKET GARDENS

Steampacket Gardens, Waterfront Geelong - every first Sunday, 10.00am to 3.00pm

Photo: John Gollings

GEELONG GALLERY

The Geelong Gallery is one of the oldest and largest regional galleries in Australia, and it holds a number of Australia's most important and popular art treasures. There is an outstanding collection of 19th and early 20th century Australian paintings. The gallery is constantly changing exhibitions featuring a full spectrum of art forms, including painting, sculpture, ceramics, decorative arts, photography and works on paper. **Entry**: free

Where: Little Malop St. **Tel:** (03) 5229 3645
Open: 10 am to 5 pm, Mon to Fri; 1 pm to 5 pm, Sat, Sun and public holidays
Email: geelart@geelonggallery.org.au **www.geelonggallery.org.au**

BUSHWALKING & CYCLING

BUSHWALKING

There are limited, but very enjoyable, bushwalking opportunities in the Geelong region. There are well developed cycling/walking tracks along the Barwon River, especially from Queen's Park and Buckley Falls. The Bellarine Rail Trail is also a possibility, but better suited to bikes (though not racing bikes; see section under Cycling). More challenging walks can be tackled in the You Yangs (see the Parks & Reserves section), the Barrabool Hills and the Brisbane Ranges (see the Parks & Reserves section). Low tide beach walks from Point Lonsdale through to Torquay - and beyond on the Surf Coast Walk - are outstanding.

CYCLING

There are a limited number of cycling tracks in the region, including along the Barwon River between Batesford and the Moorabool St Bridge, and the Bellarine Rail Trail.

BELLARINE RAIL TRAIL

The Bellarine Rail Trail follows the old railway line 33 km between Geelong and Queenscliff, and has been designed with walkers, joggers, horse riders and cyclists in mind. The railway was opened in 1879 to service the military fort at Queenscliff, and was closed to regular services in 1976. The Bellarine Peninsula Railway's vintage trains still run on the section between Queenscliff and Drysdale and carry passengers on Sundays and public holidays.

The rail trail begins near the Geelong Showgrounds, about one km from the South Geelong railway station and ends near the historic Queenscliff railway station. It is mainly flat, with some short, steep climbs up from Leopold toward Curlewis and Drysdale. Steam trains still run on the section between Queenscliff and Drysdale. There are many access points to the trail and bay scenery and birdlife are some of the highlights. The 2.5 metre wide trail is constructed of compacted, crushed rock and provides a high quality surface suitable for all bikes other than those fitted with racing tyres.

BELLARINE CIRCUIT

Road warriors might like to consider a circuit of the Peninsula, using back roads where possible. Distances:

- Geelong to Drysdale - 20.7km
- Drysdale to Portarlington - 9.7km
- Portarlington to Indented Head - 7.9km
- Indented Heads to St Leonards - 2.8km
- St Leonards to Queenscliff - 23.6km
- Queenscliff to Ocean Grove 19.6km
- Ocean Grove to Barwon Heads - 3.7km
- Barwon Heads to Breakwater Road 20.4km

Left: Joe Mortelliti, 13th Beach
Above: Bruce Kirby, Balyang Sanctuary

Top: George Stawicki, 13th Beach
Bottom: George Stawicki, Barwon Heads Golf Club
Right: George Stawicki, Torquay

GOLF

The Bellarine Peninsula has an outstanding selection of golf courses including two – the Barwon Heads Golf Club, and 13th Beach Golf Club - that are rated in Australia's Top 20. There are a large number of others, some of them of very high quality – although they are also considerably less expensive - sufficient to keep a demanding golfer out of trouble (or could that be in trouble?) for a long time.

BARWON HEADS GOLF CLUB

Barwon Heads Golf Club is a links in the Scottish tradition, on the western edge of Barwon Heads, fronting onto the dunes of 13th Beach. There are magnificent views from the undulating fairways and the wind and natural hazards provide a test of golfing skill despite its relatively short length. The club was founded in 1907, and the present site was first developed in 1920. The grand old club house (a favourite with the Western District and Geelong elite) was built in 1924.

Where: Golf Links Rd, Barwon Heads

Tel: 03 Phone (03) 5254 2302

Specs: 18 Holes, Par 70, 5757m

13TH BEACH GOLF CLUB

The 13th Beach Golf Club has two new courses that form the centerpiece of a new residential development on the outskirts of Barwon Heads. The Beach Course was the first course to open (in 2001) and has received glowing reviews. It was designed by Tony Cashmore in association with Nick Faldo, and is picturesque, rugged and challenging. Faldo has been quoted as saying, 'players who want to post a great score will require a strategy to get around it.'

Where: Barwon Heads Rd, Barwon Heads

Tel: (03) 5254 1097

Specs: 18 holes, Par 72

THE SANDS GOLF CLUB

The Sands, at Torquay, will almost certainly join the top rank of Australian courses when it opens. The design is by Australian Stuart Appleby, and it takes full advantage of the beautiful stretch of coastal hinterland to the west of Torquay.

Tel: (03) 5264 8888

BELLARINE LAKES GOLF CLUB

A challenging course featuring water hazards on a number of holes; there's great birdlife on the adjoining Reedy Lakes wetlands.

Where: Bellarine Hwy, Moolap

Tel: (03) 5250 3891

Specs: 18 holes, Par 72, 6001 metres

Top: George Stawicki, Swan Island
Bottom: Richard Everist, Avalon

GOLF

CLIFTON SPRINGS GOLF CLUB

An undulating course with magnificent views over Corio Bay – that demands accuracy. It's highly rated and moderately priced.

Where: Clearwater Drive, Clifton Springs.

Tel: (03) 5253 1488

CURLEWIS GOLF CLUB

A challenging course on rolling terrain, Curlewis offers a taste of British heath land golf with wide rolling fairways and large, fast greens.

Where: Portarlington Road, Drysdale

Tel: Phone (03) 5251 2534

Specs: 18 holes, Par 72, 6142 metres

LONSDALE GOLF CLUB

A challenging short course, on sand, surrounded by ti-tree, notable for the birdlife and proximity to Lake Victoria; there are fast greens and tricky winds.

Where: 69 Fellows Rd, Pt Lonsdale

Tel: (03) 5258 1955

Specs: 18 holes, Par 72, 5807 metres

PORTARLINGTON GOLF CLUB

Portarlington is a tree lined, challenging course with wonderful variety and excellent, fast greens.

Where: Hood Road, Portarlington

Tel: (03) 5259 2492

Specs: 18 holes, Par 72, 6035 metres

QUEENSCLIFF GOLF CLUB

Tucked away out of sight on Swan Island this peaceful course is excellent in wet weather; there are ti-tree challenges combined with a tranquil setting surrounded by water.

Where: Swan Island, Queenscliff

Tel: (03) 5258 1951

Specs: 18 Holes, Par 72, 5873 metres

QUEENS PARK GOLF COURSE

Mostly flat, but set on a scenic bend of the Barwon River, surrounded by steep escarpments; modest cost and busy at weekends.

Where: Queens Park Road, Newtown

Tel: (03) 5221 3592

Specs: 18 Holes, Par 66, 4640 metres

Top: Joe Mortelliti, Limeburners' Point
Bottom: Richard Everist, Corio Bay
Right: Natalie Russel, Corio Bay

FISHING

From a fishing point of view, a healthy bay means good fishing... Fortunately the Bay is remarkably healthy given the large human population that surrounds it and its slow water exchange with Bass Strait.

Recent research attributes significant credit for the health of the Bay to the enormous number and diversity of bottom-dwelling fauna. Flushing times vary from 260 days in the middle of the Bay, to 350 days at the Geelong end of Corio Bay but thanks to its shallowness (averaging less than 13 metres) light penetrates to the bottom promoting the proliferation of micro-organisms and invertebrates that clean the water. Intriguingly, many of the invertebrates burrow up to 50 cm for food, which has the effect of increasing the water-sediment interface, enabling oxygen to penetrate the murk and, through a complicated process, neutralizing dangerous nitrates.

Like all natural systems, the Bay's is delicately poised. Fortunately scallop dredging is no longer permitted so there has been some recovery of the sea grasses (and the scallops), although there has also been a proliferation of marine pests introduced in the ballast of incoming cargo vessels. Nonetheless, the Bay is a rich fishing ground for flathead (the ugliest species, most numerous and unfashionable, but delicious), and nobler varieties like trevally, whiting, bream – and the king of them all, the snapper.

SNAPPER

One of the best known and most highly prized species of saltwater fish in southern Australian waters, the snapper was given its name by Captain James Cook in 1770. Australian snapper belong to the family of breams or porgies and its closest relative in Victoria is the black bream. In Victoria they can grow to 16kg.

Corio Bay is a key destination on the mysterious spring snapper migration that annually unfolds across Port Phillip and Westernport Bays. No-one knows where the snapper go in March, although tagged fish have been found as far away as the South Australian border. However, sometime between September and November, moving to a timetable humans do not read, tens of thousands of snapper follow some primordial instinct and migrate from the ocean into the bays. Some spawn, although even this part of the lifecycle is a mystery.

MULLOWAY

The estuary of the Barwon River has a large variety of fish including flathead, salmon, mullet, trevally and bream. However, the greatest prize is the elusive mulloway, sometimes known as the ghost of the estuary. It is the ultimate prize in estuary fishing and can grow to 60kg, although it is more commonly around caught at seven to 35 kg. Mulloway do not reach sexual maturity until they are nearly 20 years old.

Top: Judy Scanlon, Bells Beach
Bottom: Judy Scanlon, Winkipop
Right: Judy Scanlon, Rip Curl Pro

SURFING

Surfing is part of the life-blood of Geelong and the Bellarine Peninsula, with some of the best waves on the planet a 20 minute drive from the centre of Geelong. Torquay is the gateway to the Surf Coast, and home to a remarkable concentration of internationally-famous surf brands, including Quiksilver, Piping Hot and Rip Curl.

Bells Beach (see separate section, **Parks & Reserves**) is one of the surfing world's iconic breaks and is host to the world's longest-running professional competition, the Easter Rip Curl Pro. Surfers will find that quality waves can be found the length of the peninsula.

HISTORY

Surfing at Bells began in the late 1940s, but the beach was extremely inaccessible and the boards of the time (16 feet long and wooden) were not easy to transport. The sport was given a crucial boost in 1956 when, in conjunction with the Melbourne Olympic Games, an International Surf Life Saving Carnival was held at Torquay in front of enormous crowds. The competing teams included one from Hawaii, managed by the great Duke Kahanamoku, that brought revolutionary fiberglass Malibu boards for wave riding.

This was the first time that Malibu boards had been seen by large numbers of people, and most of them were sold to enthusiastic Australians. Over the next few years there was considerable experimentation with balsawood and foam – and a keen group of Torquay surfers starting surfing Bells on a regular basis. The group included Peter Troy, Joe Sweeney, 'China' Gilbert and 'Ming' Smith. The first contest at Bells – with a 1 pound prize – was held in 1961 and won by 'Ming' Smith.

A growing number of young Australian fell in love with the sport, and following the short board revolution of 1967 a number of fanatics started surf-related businesses in garages and derelict shops around Torquay –hoping to make a living, but more importantly to do a lot of surfing. Among them were Doug Warbrick and Brian Singer of Rip Curl, and Alan Green and John Law of Quiksilver.

Rip Curl started making surfboards in a competitive market that included many great names (Pat Morgan and Fred Pyke among many others), and in 1970 began making the first primitive surfing wetsuits: the product that has been the backbone of their company ever since. Quiksilver started with a revolutionary new design for boardshorts and went on to produce sheepskin boots and a range of surf-wear. Piping Hot started in 1975 with wetsuits and has also moved on to clothing. It's curious to see these developments in the context of Geelong's long textile tradition…
All three companies are now multinational icons.

Top: Judy Scanlon, Winkipop
Bottom: Judy Scanlon, Winkipop
Right: Artist Photographer, Winkipop

SURF BREAKS

After a south-westerly storm has pushed through the Great Southern Ocean and a high pressure system has started to generate its first gentle northerlies, it can be difficult to find a self-employed tradie on the job anywhere on the Peninsula. These are the conditions local surfers pray for – but if you're not fussy, as long as the wind is not from the south or east, chances are there'll be a rideable wave somewhere on the Peninsula.

- There are fierce left handers at **Glaneuse** at **Point Lonsdale**, on the edge of the Rip, and some heavy shore-breaks (great for body surfing) as well.
- **Ocean Grove** and **Raff's** (nearer the Barwon Heads Bridge) have some pleasant beach-break rollers ideal for beginners.
- **13th Beach** is a good option on a small swell, but it can also hold a serious left and right-hand wave at **Beacon**; the wave size drops off towards Bancoora with a range of enjoyable beach breaks.
- **Bancoora Reef** can be outstanding on a good day.
- The nice slow right-hander 'inside' at **Point Impossible** (or **Possos**) can get crowded, but 'river mouth' and 'outside' (the outer reef) are rarely busy; be prepared for a long paddle if the outer reef appeals.
- **Torquay** can hold a wave on the point, but Jan Juc's beach breaks are generally more rewarding.
- **Jan Juc** has good quality beach breaks (another option on a small swell) – but the local grommets are a greedy bunch.
- After Jan Juc there are a number of breaks, like **Bird Rock**, which are haunted by locals.
- The best wave on the coast is a fast, steep right-hander at **Winkipop**, which is accessed from the Bell's Beach car park, but separated from the better known Bells Beach, by a rock outcrop know as 'the button'.
- **Bells** has several surfable sections of reef and can hold a very large, fast wave, but it also has a number of slower, fatter, 'classic' sections.

Top: Robert Bole, Bells Beach
Bottom: Artist Photographer, Eastern Beach

DIVING & SNORKELING

The diving and snorkeling around the Bellarine Peninsula is outstanding, and Port Phillip Heads is often rated among the top ten dive sites in the world. There are over 12,000 species of plants and animals in the waters around the Peninsula, ranging from spectacular algal communities and colourful inverte-brates to seals, dolphins and whales.

Recognising this extraordinary resource, there are now a number of important marine national parks and marine sanctuaries (see separate **Parks & Reserves** section). Most important is the Port Phillip Heads Marine National Park. In the Rip, spectacular wall and drift dives show colour and diversity rivalling that on the Great Barrier Reef, with bull kelp, sponge gardens and soft corals. And the Lonsdale Reef has at least four visible and recognisable shipwrecks: the iron sailing barques George Roper, Holyhead and Gange, and the gold rush steamer Conside.

For beginners, the sheltered rock pools at Point Lonsdale provide easy snorkeling. There are also beginner's tours from Queenscliff that take in Pope's Eye and Chinaman's Hat. Originally built as a fortress, Pope's Eye is now a rookery for the Australian Gannet and there is a protected lagoon where it is possible to snorkel safely and observe kelp and brightly coloured fish. Chinaman's Hat is a purpose-built seal platform where visitors can snorkel with the locals: curious, playful, Australian fur seals.

Some wonderful creatures are unique to southern Australian waters, famously the weird Weedy Seadragon, Victoria's marine state emblem. Weedy Seadragons are from the same family as seahorses and pipefish are often found in Victoria's kelp forests where their unusual body shape allows them to hide amongst the seaweeds. With their highly modified fins that resemble seaweed, these animals are beautifully camouflaged, despite their bright colours. If anything is weirder, it's the highly coloured Nudibranchs –there are 400 species in Australian waters. Another favourite with divers is the Western Blue Devilfish, its vivid sapphire body and iridescent blue spots contrasting with the reds, oranges and yellows of sponge gardens.

Top: George Stawicki, Barwon Bluff
Bottom: George Stawicki, Bells Beach
Right: Judy Scanlon, Bells Beach

PARKS & RESERVES

BARWON BLUFF MARINE SANCTUARY

Known to the Wathaurong as Kolo:oit, the Bluff at the mouth of the Barwon River, was an important meeting and camping area for thousands of years. The Wathaurong's bark shelters have been replaced by a picturesque football ground, caravans and prefabs, but it is still a great place to camp: sheltered and shady, with great fishing and a reef teeming with life. The caravan park and jetty were the setting for the ABC television programme Sea Change.

The Bluff is formed from calcenarite, the remains of an old dune formed on top of a lava flow from Mt Duneed. There are great views from the top looking eastwards towards the Rip and beyond to Cape Schanck, westwards towards Torquay and the Otways, north across the Barwon estuary to the You Yangs.

At the tip of the bluff a pincer-shaped reef juts into the sea; the eastern pincer is basalt from Mt Duneed, the western is sandstone and has been eroded into arches and gutters. The eastern reef is under the influence of the river and supports filter-feeding animals like feather-stars, and the western reef has weathered into ledges and pools that shelter sea slugs and a large variety of other animals, including abalone and rock lobsters. Between the reef pincers there's a small bay, regularly visited by rays and just offshore there are beds of giant kelp and sponges.

BELLS BEACH SURFING RECREATION RESERVE

Bells Beach Surfing Recreation Reserve is administered by Surf Coast Shire, recognising that Bells, has become a legendary surf spot. Even if it were not the location for the world's oldest professional surfing competition, it's only necessary to witness one big swell and Bells will engrave itself on your memory forever: majestic lines of swell marching in from the Southern Ocean and peeling mechanically across the bay to Winkipop.

Offshore the reserve is part of the new Point Addis Marine National Park, which stretches west to Anglesea, taking in a number of reefs. The Surf Coast Walk, which starts at the Jan Juc car park and continues all the way to Mogg's Creek (past Aireys Inlet), passes through the car park at Bells. Two easy and enjoyable stretches include Bells to Jan Juc (4 km, 1 hour) or a spectacular section through the Ironbark Basin to the Point Addis Car Park (5 km, 1.75 hours).

Top: Joe Mortelliti, Brisbane Ranges
Bottom: Joe Mortelliti, Rowsley, Brisbane Ranges
Right: Robert Bole, Brisbane Ranges

BRISBANE RANGES NATIONAL PARK

The Brisbane Ranges National Park, the only national park in the region, is a little known gem, 30 km north-west of Geelong. A visit to the park can be combined with time spent pottering around the Historic Park at Steiglitz, or the vineyards or Fairy Park at Anakie.

The Brisbane Ranges stretch from Bacchus Marsh in the north to Maude in the south. Although only 400 metres high, there are good views over the Werribee plains and the eastern part of the park is cut by steep gorges.

The park is considered to be particularly significant for its wildflowers and flora: 61 species of orchids and a total of 619 species of vascular plants have been recorded. It also includes a moving historical legacy.

It is believed small bands of Wathaurong regularly occupied the ranges. The country to the west along the Moorabool River was settled early and in 1859 a number of the remaining Wathaurong were relocated to the Steiglitz Reserve. The reserve was hardly used however, and was closed in 1901; there is a comm-emorative plaque at the Little River Picnic Area.

The most dramatic impact on the ecology of the region was caused by the discovery and mining of gold at Steiglitz from 1851. By 1862 there were over 600 miners in the region and large amounts of timber were harvested to supply Steiglitz with timber for mine shoring, construction and other domestic uses. The mines around Steiglitz fell into disuse in the early 1900s and the town is now effectively a ghost town, with only a few key buildings surviving. Dry-stone walls, mine shafts, mullock heaps and foundations can still be seen in many parts of the park.

In spring there is a magnificent display of wattles, hakeas and bush peas. There are forests of Stringybark, Ironbark and Manna Gum. Koalas are common, along with Grey Kangaroos, Red-necked Wallabies, echidnas, possums and gliders. Birdlife includes the endangered Swift Parrot, Powerful Owl and Painted Honeyeater.

Most of the walking in the park is fairly rugged. There is a popular three-day walk from Boar Gully Camping Area to Steiglitz known as the Burchell Trail (permits required; tel 5284 1230). There are also shorter, easier day walks: the Anakie Gorge Walk (3 km, 2 hours) follows the route of the pipeline constructed in 1870 that carried water from the Stony Creek Reservoir to Geelong; the Ted Errey Nature Circuit (8 km, 3 hours) from the Stony Creek Picnic Area is a good introduction to the regions flora and has several excellent viewpoints; the Wadawurrung Walk (2.5 km, 1 hour) has good views of the You Yangs and Anakie Gorge.

Top: Artist Photographer, Lake Connewarre
Bottom: Artist Photographer, Lake Connewarre

EDWARD POINT STATE FAUNAL RESERVE

Edward Point State Faunal Reserve is near St Leonards on the Bellarine Peninsula; it protects the sand spit and a small island that shelter the waters and salt marsh of the Swan Bay Reserve.

There are several vegetation communities including coastal tea-tree, saltbush and swampier areas with swamp weed and glasswort. Swamp weed is a typical salt marsh plant identified by its pale fan-like flowers in summer and bright green spoon-shaped leaves up to 10cm long. In the middle of the spit, the bush opens out and gives way to coastal grassland with occasional small clumps of trees and shrubs (commonly Coast Beard-heath and Wirilda).

The birdlife is significant. Along the beach there are likely to be groups of tiny Red-necked Stints feeding at the waters edge. White-fronted Chats, Crested Terns and Pied Oyster-catchers are also commonly seen. On the Swan Bay side a number of waders, and possibly even Orange-bellied Parrots, can be seen.

Access to the reserve is via Beach Rd. From Geelong, take the Portarlington Road; turn off at Murradoc Road; then turn into Bluff Road, right at Cliff Street, then left at Beach Road.

LAKE CONNEWARRE STATE GAME RESERVE

Lake Connewarre is a large lake just inland from the estuary of the Barwon River. It forms a fascinating wetland environment that has been recognised as internationally significant under the Ramsar Convention. (The Convention on Wetlands, signed in Ramsar, Iran, in 1971, is an intergovernmental treaty aimed at conserving important of wetlands.) The word Connewarre is thought to be derived from an aboriginal word for black swan.

The reserve is made up of a permanent freshwater lake, a deep freshwater marsh and several semi-permanent saline wetlands, as well as the Barwon estuary. The lake is critically important to migrant and domestic bird populations (72 water bird species have been recorded) and to fish populations, as a habitat and nursery.

The reserve also supports 40% of the world population of the endangered Orange-bellied Parrot. Unfortunately it is under growing pressure because of pollution and weak water flows in the Barwon, and from the rapidly expanding housing developments at Leopold. Lake Connewarre has high vegetation richness, with 137 native plants, including the most extensive herb and grasslands.

The Lake can be accessed from Brinsmead Lane, off the Bellarine Hwy (just east of Leopold), or from Lake Rd, off the Barwon Heads Rd (beside the airport).

Top: Richard Everist, You Yangs
Bottom: Joe Mortelliti, You Yangs

LITTLE RIVER EARTH SANCTUARY

The Little River Earth Sanctuary was created to provide the endangered wildlife of Victoria's western plains a quality habitat, protected from feral animals. This important concept – of a feral-animal free sanctuary – first developed by Dr John Wamsley at Warrawong Earth Sanctuary in the Adelaide Hills, has now been replicated at three other properties around Australia: at Little River, on Kangaroo Island and in the Blue Mountains outside Sydney.

The Little River Earth Sanctuary was formally known as Mt Rothwell and was part of the Chirnside family's enormous pastoral holdings (which included Werribee Park).

Earth Sanctuaries Ltd bought the Mt Rothwell property – including the historic homestead - from the Chirnsides in 2000, and it was opened to the public in 2002. The 1185 ha property has now been surrounded by 21 km of feral animal–proof fencing and a number of threatened species have been, or are in the process of being, reintroduced.

The sanctuary property is situated at the northern end of the You Yangs, 30 minutes from Geelong. The elevated site has excellent views of the Melbourne skyline, the You Yangs, Brisbane Ranges and Port Phillip Bay. An important feature is a 200 ha remnant of old-growth grassy woodland, but an active volunteer group is helping to restore the natural habitats.

Long-nosed Potoroos, Southern Brown Bandicoots, Rufous Bettongs, Red-bellied Pademelons, Eastern Quolls and Brush-tailed Phascogales have been introduced back to their former range, with some species not seen in the wild in Victoria for 50 to 100 years.

A stunning feature of the property is a heritage-listed 130-year-old bluestone homestead formally owned by the Chirnside family. The homestead is a single storied, simple Italianate style, bluestone building containing 25 rooms and covering about 90 squares. The residence is an intact example of a wealthy pastoral home that still displays rare decorative schemes.

The sanctuary is open daily - with prior booking - for guided walks. Bookings are essential; phone 5283 1602. It is recommended you wear sturdy footwear and bring a hat, camera, small torch (for the sunset walk) and sunscreen.

The **Wildlife Adventure Walk** departs at sunset and is a two hour walk designed to explore the sanctuary and animals thriving in an old-growth grassy woodland. The cost is $22 for adults, $17.50 for children, and $59.50 for families.

The **Historic Mt Rothwell Homestead Tour** departs at 4 pm and is a one-hour exploration of the heritage Chirnside homestead and garden. The cost is $10 per person.

On Sundays only, you can also book for a **Ned Kelly Film Set Tour**. It departs at 3 pm, and you see the recreated village of Greta from the 2003 feature film. The cost is $15 for adults, $10 for children, and $45 for families.

Top: Barry Feldman, Point Danger
Bottom: George Stawicki, Point Danger
Right: Bruce Kirby, Coast

OCEAN GROVE NATURE RESERVE

The Ocean Grove Nature Reserve is extremely important as it is among the last, remnant bushland on the Bellarine Peninsula. Covering a mere 143 ha, the land was purchased in the 1960s, thanks to fundraising by a dedicated group of locals. Despite the small area, there are several distinct vegetation communities; the most prominent is an area of Grass-tree, Manna Gum, Yellow Gum, and the beautiful Drooping Sheoak. Black Sheoak and several species of wattle are prominent.

Over 130 species of bird have been recorded; most prominent among the residents are the Eastern Rosella. Mammals include the Red-necked Wallaby and Echidna. One unusual rarity is a small blue butterfly which breeds in ant nests. There is a network of walking tracks and bird observation hides at appropriate sites.

The reserve is on the west side of Grubb Rd, between the Bellarine Highway and Ocean Grove, 25 km south-east of Geelong.

POINT DANGER MARINE SANCTUARY

Point Danger at Torquay is found at the meeting point of the surf and front beaches. Once considered a navigational hazard to sailing ships, today, the reef is considered just another part of this beautiful and wild coastline. Point Danger is very popular for sightseeing and shore walks, and is visited by large numbers of people. The point is also a popular surf break. Snorkeling around Point Danger is a great way to see some of the diversity of the area.

In 1891 the reef was struck by a three-masted sailing ship, the Joseph H. Scammell. No lives were lost, but the cargo, including kerosene, hardware, and rolls of tobacco was scattered for miles. The valuable wreckage sparked off the largest wave of illegal looting, pilfering and smuggling in the Geelong area's history when thousands scoured the beaches for loot. The pine deckhouse was used to build the lower portion of Scammel House which can still be seen in Pride St, Torquay.

As well as containing a typically high invertebrate diversity associated with limestone reefs in Victoria, about 20% of the 96 species of sea slugs recorded from this site have not yet been scientifically described. Keyhole limpets, crabs and mussels are abundant. Banded Brittle stars and carnivorous worms emerge from under rocks to feed at nightly high tides. The site is also known for its diversity of sea slugs known as opisthobranchs, which unlike the garden slug, appears here in a range of exquisite shapes, colours and sizes. On the sides of the reef, brown seaweeds with zigzag stems grow profusely on the rocks, giving way to bright green seagrass beds covering the sand Eagle Rays patrol the outer reef edge.

Top: George Stawicki, The Rip
Bottom: George Stawicki, Point Lonsdale
Right: Joe Mortelliti, The Heads

PORT PHILLIP HEADS MARINE NATIONAL PARK

The Port Phillip Heads Marine National Park includes Port Phillip Heads, and is made up of six separate areas including Swan Bay, Great Sands (Mud Islands), Point Lonsdale, Point Nepean, Popes Eye and Portsea Hole incorporating a total of 3,580 hectares.

Habitat types found within the park include seagrass beds, sheltered mudflats, sandy beaches and rocky shores, and rocky reefs, as well as the open water environment. There is an extraordinary diversity and abundance of marine flora and fauna.

The high diversity of marine life is due to the wide range of habitats in the area and its central Victorian location. The area marks the end of the range for some animals and plants that prefer the cold waters of western Victoria, but it also supports species from eastern Australia that can survive in the bay's relatively calm, warm, shallow waters. A high proportion of Victorian species of marine flora and fauna are represented in the Port Phillip Head's region.

The region which now is covered by the Port Phillip Heads Marine National Park, has a long history of use by both the Aboriginal inhabitants of this region as well as featuring significantly in early European settlement and migration.

There are a number of significant sites adjacent to the Marine National Park where the remains of shellfish and other animals are found in large numbers, in what are referred to as shell middens. Midden sites are all protected as they provide an important record of the rich cultural history of indigenous Victorians and the coast.

As the gateway to the bay, the heads have always been the eye of a needle on a vital shipping route. A vast number of ships have threaded their way through the heads, but a number have come to grief on the hidden reefs at the narrow entrance. Some of these wrecks are now found within the Port Phillip Heads Marine National Park. These include the Holyhead, George Roper and Conside on the Lonsdale Reef. The Eliza Ramsden near Point Nepean and the William Salthouse, an important wreck near Popes Eye, lie near the park.

The heads have also traditionally been seen as vital to Victoria's security; defence has been a preoccupation since the earliest days of the colony. Melbournians paid for the construction of a number of forts, some of which are still used by the Department of Defence. Within the Marine National Park, Popes Eye was established as the base of a fortress that was never completed – but other fortifications, including the South Channel Fort and extensive fortifications at both Point Nepean and Queenscliff were completed. The rocks placed on the sand bar at Popes Eye were soon colonised by kelp and many other plants and animals, and today the site is considered one of the most important dive and snorkeling sites in the Bay.

Top: George Stawicki, Swan Bay
Bottom: George Stawicki, sand banks
Right: Joe Mortelliti, Pelican

SWAN BAY

The natural values of Swan Bay are of regional, national and international significance. The tidal mudflats and surrounding fringe of salt marsh support large numbers of wader birds including many that migrate from the Northern Hemisphere during summer months.

The expanse of tidal seagrass beds is a major nursery habitat for many species of fish, including leather jackets, flounder, King George whiting, black bream, garfish and flathead. Forty-four fish species have been recorded in Swan Bay. The importance of Swan Bay as a fish nursery area has long been recognised by Queenscliff fishermen and it was protected unofficially for nearly 100 years, before being officially protected under legislation in 1970.

In addition, the seagrass provides food to black swans, and the surrounding area provides a breeding ground for spoonbills, cormorants and egrets. The endangered Orange-bellied Parrot uses the salt marshes fringing Swan Bay as a winter refuge and feeding ground.

MUD ISLANDS (GREAT SANDS)

The Mud Islands, approximately 6 km north-east of Portsea, are an exposed section of the Great Sands, the most extensive sandbank in the Bay. Reminiscent in some ways of a coral cay, they consist of three shrubby sand islands, enclosing a shallow tidal lagoon, which is fringed by salt marsh. The island group has a total land area of 60 hectares and reaches a height of four metres.

Formed by wind and wave action, the Mud Islands are anchored by outcrops of phosphate rock. This rare rock forms below guano (bird droppings) when phosphate leaches down and combines with shelly sand to form a hard calcium phosphate. This rock is resistant to erosion, thus creating an ideal nesting site for birds whose droppings continue to keep the whole system going. The major species is silver gulls - with an estimated forty to fifty thousand pairs, this is one of the largest colonies in the world. Other species include straw-necked ibis, and white ibis. In summer the central lagoon is visited by thousands of intercontinental waders. Altogether some 70 species have been recorded.

The Mud Islands support a distinctive community of animals that live in the sand. This is an important habitat for numerous invertebrate species, including small crustaceans and segmented worms. These invertebrates provide an important source of food for many fish and birds. Dense seagrass beds growing over the sand and mudflats provide vital breeding, foraging and nursery areas for many fish such as King George whiting. These sandy soft sediments also provide habitat for scallops, mussels, oysters and many bottom-dwelling fish. Many of these bottom-dwelling fish species, including yank, sand flathead and snapper, also rely on animals that live in the soft sediment habitat for food.

Flounder and other fish flourish in the shallow sandy habitats and a number of shark species use these areas for basking. During summer months, Bronze Whaler sharks use the warm waters around Mud Islands to give birth to their young.

POINT LONSDALE

The Point Lonsdale component of the park includes excellent examples of the diverse physical and biological features of the area, including spectacular deep-water scenery featuring cliffs, caverns, rocky reef walls, sponge gardens and kelp beds.

Many of the rocks that make up this reef as well as rocks and cliffs above the water are made of ancient dune limestone or calcarenite. This readily weathered rock is made of sand grains that have been cemented together by calcium carbonate from dissolved shells. The Rip side of Point Lonsdale contains an extensive rocky platform covered with algae such as Neptune's Necklace, and has a number of larger rock pools suitable for snorkeling.

The reefs offshore from Point Lonsdale provide spectacular underwater terrain with ledges, rock outcrops and bommies, and beds of bull kelp on sections exposed to large waves. Fishermen seeking an easier entrance to the bay through the Rip in their small fishing boats blasted a channel out of the Lonsdale Reef. The channel between the main rock platform and the outer reef is around 20 metres wide and two to four deep and contains a small forest of Giant Kelp, a species which is showing signs of decline along the south-east coast of Australia.

Giant Kelp occurs only sporadically on the Victorian coast and is of interest due to its ability to form complex forest-like habitats and also its rapid growth during winter and spring. It grows to over 10 metres in height and its upper canopy provides habitat for a range of fish and invertebrate communities.

The Lonsdale Wall is a series of ledges that mark the edge of the historical course of the Yarra River. The wall drops down a series of ledges from 15 to 90 metres depth, extending horizontally for about a kilometre. The vertical walls, sheltered caves, ledges and overhangs and their associated communities

of colourful sponges, fish and encrusting algae provide spectacular scenery and provide popular dive sites. Species include an array of sponges, soft corals, gorgonians, hydroids, jewel anemones and sea tulips and 43 species of fish.

The Sponge Gardens area contains a high diversity of sponges and other filter feeding invertebrates in a variety of colours, shapes and forms. In the main flow of current through the Rip, these animals are able to extract plankton from the water that passes by. The area derives its name from the spectacular and diverse sponges, branching soft corals, stalked ascidians and carpets of colourful anemones.

POINT NEPEAN

The Point Nepean component contains extensive shallow reefs covered in kelp and supports a variety of marine life including Victoria's marine state emblem the Weedy Seadragon, seahorses, cuttlefish and numerous algal and invertebrate species.

Top: Joe Mortelliti, Point Lonsdale
Right: Barry Feldman, Point Lonsdale

Top: Barry Feldman, 13th Beach
Bottom: Artist Photographer,13th Beach

PORTSEA HOLE

Portsea hole is a 30-metre depression within the bed of the old Yarra River that is popular with divers. It acts as a shelter for a variety of fish and other reef species and there is a fascinating stratification of marine life on the wall.

POPES EYE

Popes Eye, approximately five km north-east of Portsea, is an island made of bluestone boulders that have been laid in a semi-circular ring. Originally intended as the foundations for one of the fortresses guarding Port Phillip, but never completed, this structure provides a safe anchorage, and ideal snorkeling.

In many ways the rich community of animals and plants it shelters is a microcosm of the Heads reef environment, and as fishing has been prohibited for over 20 years fish are abundant. Fish species include wrasse, morwongs, old wives, scaly fin and perch. Australasian Gannets nest on the platform and rocks above the water and Australian Fur Seals are often seen in the area.

Inside the stone ring the water depth is only around 1.5 metres but outside the water drops to around 10 metres. There are extensive beds of kelp which create a forest like environment. Beneath the kelp there is an array of colourful encrusting algae and organisms like seastars, sponges, feather stars, sea urchins, sponges, sea squirts and soft corals adorning the rocks.

Top: Bruce Kirby
Bottom: Richard Everist, You Yangs

SERENDIP SANCTUARY

Originally developed as sheep-grazing property, Serendip was purchased by the government for use by Fisheries and Wildlife for research purposes. In 1987, the property was redeveloped as an education centre focused on the wetlands and wildlife of the Western Plains.

The re-developments included the construction of an information centre, refurbishment of existing buildings, creation of walking trails, building of bird hides and covered walkways, marshland construction and installation of displays and educational material. A picnic area with free undercover electric barbecues is provided.

The 250 ha sanctuary provides an excellent example of the open grassy woodlands and wetlands of the volcanic Western Plains and is the perfect place to experience wetlands ecology. Specially designed bird hides enable you to see the birds that breed at Serendip, or visit, at close hand. More than 150 species of bird common to the Western Plains of Victoria have been recorded.

Australian Bustards, Brolgas and Bush Thick-knees are three rare Victorian birds which were once common on the Western Plains and now find a protected home at Serendip. Brolgas and Australian Bustards were chosen for the captive breeding program, designed to rehabilitate species that have become rare or extinct on the Western Plains. The success of the captive breeding program has received international recognition.

Serendip also provides habitat for a variety of mammal species including Eastern Grey Kangaroos, Red-necked Wallabies, Swamp Wallabies, Echidnas, a limited number of Koala.

NARANA CREATIONS

Narana welcomes visitors into an Aboriginal place. The gallery/shop displays high-quality Aboriginal art and crafts – including paintings, and didgeridoos. Staff are happy to share their knowledge of history and culture as well as their practical skills with boomerangs and didgeridoos. A varied cultural programme enables groups to participate in a variety of activities including an exploration of the extensive native garden and its foods.

410 Torquay Rd, Grovedale **Entry:** free **Tel:** (03) 5241 5700

Open: 9 am to 5 pm, Mon to Fri; 10 am to 4 pm, Sat

Email: info@narana.com.au **www.narana.com.au**

YOU YANGS REGIONAL PARK

The You Yangs are a series of low granite ridges that reach 352 metres at Flinders Peak, the highest point. Despite this modest height, the You Yangs are a dramatic and inescapable landmark for miles around – from Barwon Heads, from many points along the Great Dividing Range, even from the eastern side of Port Phillip Bay. Every European explorer worth his salt – since Matthew Flinders on 1 May 1802 - has found a climb to the top an irresistible challenge. And the view is impressive.

Contrary to popular belief – and to their appearance – the You Yangs are not the remains of a volcano. The nearest volcanos are the Anakies to the west. In line with popular belief – and their appearance – the You Yangs are, however, very old. The granite that forms them worked its way through surrounding sedimentary rocks in the Devonian period, roughly 365 million years ago, long before the dinosaurs. The magma never reached the surface and cooled slowly allowing large white crystals of feldspar (which can be seen in many of the rocky outcrops) to form. Over mind-boggling aeons the surrounding land surface and sedimentary rocks have inexorably eroded away, leaving behind the granite.

The You Yangs were significant to the Wathaurong. There is no permanent water in the vicinity, so natural hollows in the granite rocks were enlarged to form wells that held water even in dry seasons (some of these can be seen on Big Rock).

A variety of plant species can be found. Tall eucalypts such as Manna Gums, Yellow Gums and River Red Gums give way to a sparse undergrowth of native shrubs and ground covers. Patches of wattles and Drooping Sheoaks can also be seen. More than 200 species of birds have been recorded in the area and mammals such as kangaroos, koalas, sugar gliders, brushtail and ringtail possums are also commonly seen.

Unfortunately, much of the original vegetation was cleared for farming, and timber plantations of Sugar Gum and Brown Mallet were established to supply local communities with firewood, and posts. On 14th January 1985, a fire burnt more than 80% of the park. The vegetation is now slowly recovering although South African Boneseed, a noxious weed, is also proliferating. Volunteer groups are actively involved in controlling its spread and research into biological controls is proceeding.

There is a Visitors' Centre and several bar-b-q areas. The Great Circle Drive is a 12 km scenic loop that takes in many features around the park. The road is unsealed but suitable for conventional vehicles. Flinders Peak Walk (3.2 km return, 1.5 hours) begins at the Turntable Car Park, and is signposted to the peak, where there is a plaque commemorating Matthew Flinders. On a clear day you can see Mount Macedon, the Brisbane Ranges, Geelong, Corio and Port Phillip Bays, Mount Martha and the Melbourne skyline. Look out for koalas in the trees below and Wedge-tailed Eagles soaring above.

Left: Joe Mortelliti, You Yangs

ORANGE-BELLIED PARROT

The Orange-bellied Parrot is a beautiful, endangered, migratory parrot that seems to have chosen a particularly difficult life! It migrates between the south coast of Australia and south-western Tasmania across Bass Strait, one of the wildest stretches of water in the world. (Nobody warned it that rising sea levels would make life so difficult!) Corio Bay and the Bellarine Peninsula, specifically the Cheetham wetlands, Swan Bay and Lake Connewarre, are host to 40% of the total population.

During the summer, the parrots live on the open coastal plains of south-west Tasmania. They feed on the seeds of various plants on these 'button-grass' plains and nest in adjacent forest. In March the birds leave south-west Tasmania and head north on a protracted and risky migration that takes up to two months.

The birds move up the west coast of Tasmania, feeding mainly on coastal grasses and the seeds of Sea Rocket, which grows directly above the high tide line. They then hop across the western islands of Bass Strait, to the Hunter Group and King Island, where their major source of food is Beaded Glasswort.

The parrots begin arriving on the Australian mainland from late March onwards. They disperse along the coast from as far east as Corner Inlet to Lake Alexandrina near Adelaide in the west. However, the main concentrations occur around Corio Bay and the Bellarine Peninsula.

The parrots that inhabit the Geelong region feed mainly in salt marshes where they favour Beaded Glasswort, Sea Heath, Austral Seablite, and Shrubby Glasswort. They also regularly visit the Queenscliff Golf Course to feed on seeding fairway grasses.

The Orange-bellied Parrot is approximately 20 cm long, a little larger than a budgerigar. Its plumage is bright grass-green above and mostly yellow below with a bright orange patch in the centre of the lower belly. It has a bright azure blue patch on the outer wing and a blue bar across the forehead above the nostrils.

An alarm call is given when the bird is disturbed or upset. It is a harsh, metallic, rapidly repeated 'zit-zit-zit', usually given while it is taking off from a perch or the ground. In level flight, a single 'tseet' note is given each time it dips. The call is one of the surest methods of identification as the appearance of the plumage often varies according to the light.

Left: Richard Everist, You Yangs
Above: Richard Everist, Avalon

Top: Artist Photographer, Gordon Institute of TAFE
Bottom: George Stawicki, Moorabool River

EDUCATION

In Geelong's early days most of the education that was available was provided by the churches, and by the end of the 1850s there were 32 private schools. Some were very small (literally) cottage industries, but they all survived – somewhat precariously – on a mixture of fees and government support.

St Joseph's College can trace its beginning back to 1854 when St Augustine's Catholic Church and schoolhouse were established on the current site. An orphanage was built alongside the school in 1857, and is still in use as the school's creative arts centre.

Geelong Grammar School started in 1855 in Villamanta St, and will celebrate its 150th birthday in 2005. After outgrowing a number of smaller sites, in 1858 the school moved to a new building at the corner of Moorabool and McKillop streets, part of which still stands in Maud St. The first foundation stone at the new Corio site was laid in 1913 and until 1922 students from Geelong went to and from the school by motorboat.

In 1858 the Flinders National School, a forerunner of modern state schools and now Matthew Flinders Girls Secondary College, was opened. In 1860 the Sisters of Mercy established Sacred Heart College, on the site it still occupies. Buildings still in use date back to 1863. Geelong College was opened the next year in Skene St and the beautiful Aphrasia St, Newtown site has buildings dating from 1871.

In 1872 the state government introduced laws making education compulsory and free, and the existing, largely church-based system, was converted to a system of State Schools. Mowbray's School became Ashby State School in 1875, St James' Anglican School in Newtown became Newtown State School in 1877, St Peter's Wesleyan School became Chilwell State School in 1878, Christ Church and a Wesleyan school were combined at South Geelong State School in 1879, and Flinders became a State School in 1880. In each case, beautiful old school buildings survive and are used daily.

In 1887 the Gordon Memorial Technical College (now the Gordon Institute of TAFE) was opened in memory of General Charles Gordon, a hero of the British Empire who died in the Siege of Khartoum (Sudan). In 1971 the Gordon opened a new campus at Waurn Ponds, and degree courses were offered for the first time.

In 1977 the Gordon's Waurn Ponds campus became the new Deakin University. Deakin has become famous for the distinctiveness of its courses, and especially for its focus on distance learning. There are now six campuses: three in Melbourne, two in Geelong and one in Warrnambool. The second Geelong campus is housed in one of the old wool stores on the edge of Corio Bay that was abandoned by industry. The move has helped revitalize Geelong's city centre and waterfront.

Top: Geelong Gallery, George Stawicki, courtesy Geelong Gallery
Bottom: Geelong Gallery, John Gollings, courtesy Geelong Gallery
Right: Geelong Gallery, George Stawicki, courtesy Geelong Gallery

GEELONG GALLERY

The Geelong Gallery is one of the oldest and largest of Australia's regional art galleries and it holds a number of Australia's most important and popular art treasures. Established in 1896 and situated in the heart of Geelong's arts precinct, the gallery is next to Geelong's City Hall, overlooking Johnstone Park.

The gallery is housed in a building that has undergone several extensions and refurbishments. The original gallery entrance, facing Johnstone Park, is classical revival in style, as are the principal rooms that house the outstanding collection of 19th and early 20th century Australian paintings and the smaller but by no means inconsequential collection of European (mostly British) paintings of the same period.

Although the collection itself was inaugurated in 1896, the construction of the present building did not begin until 1913. The Geelong architectural firm of Laird and Buchan was responsible for the initial phases, while the most recent development, based on a $2 million Federation Grant, was awarded to another prominent Geelong firm, McGlashan Everist.

The greatest strengths of the gallery's permanent holdings are colonial paintings, including a large number of early images of Geelong and its environs (oil and watercolour paintings, drawings and engravings); a selection of important late-nineteenth century paintings by Buvelot, McCubbin, Streeton, Withers, John Ford Paterson, Piguenit, Ashton and Roberts among others; colonial metalwork; English porcelain; works on paper (historical and modern); and modern Australian art including significant examples of sculpture and works by

prominent painters including Fred Williams, Lesley Dumbrell, Paul Partos, John Firth-Smith, Jenny Watson, Peter Booth, Juan Davila, and John Brack.

Individual highlights of the Australian collection are paintings by Eugene von Guérard including *The Barter* (1854) known variously as *The Barwon River, Geelong or Aborigines met on the way to the diggings, Mr. Levien's Hut on the Barwon River* (1860), and *The Weatherboard Falls* (1863, the gift of Alfred Felton); McCubbin's elegiac *A Bush Burial* (1890, the first acquisition by public subscription); *A breezy day off Point Henry* (1901) by Withers, arguably one of the artist's most lyrical and arresting works; and Julian Ashton's sympathetic study of a fellow painter, his *Portrait of Louis Buvelot* (1880).

Of the smaller European collection, the following works stand out: *The pier head* (1910) by Stanhope Forbes, *A Babylonian maid* (1883) by Edwin Long, *Reading the Bible* (c. 1840-45) by Thomas Faed, and On the Thames (1878) by Benjamin Leader. These are among the finest, most characteristic paintings by each of these prominent British artists. *The pier head* represents Stanhope Forbes at his bravura best. *A Babylonian maid* by Edwin Long is justly famous as one of the most important academic paintings in Australia. And the painting by Thomas Faed is an extremely fine example of the kind of Victorian narrative painting that has swung wildly in and out of fashion for much of the last century.

The gallery hosts an ambitious program of exhibitions, lectures and related events. Major events in the calendar are the *Fletcher Jones Art Prize* and the *Geelong Print Prize*, the latter supported by the gallery's entrepreneurial support group known as the *Grasshoppers*. The gallery also has an active *Friends* organisation whose members meet every month for social gatherings and lectures by visiting artists, curators and scholars.

The gallery's exhibition program features a wide-ranging selection of historical and modern offerings, covering the full spectrum of art forms from painting and sculpture to works on paper and ceramics, from textiles to photography, from architectural design to botanical illustration. Several prospective exhibitions explore aspects of local and environmental history as seen through the eyes of visual artists.

Entry: free

Open: 10 am to 5 pm, Mon to Fri; 1 pm to 5 pm Sat, Sun and public holidays

Where: Little Malop St

Tel: 5229 3645

www.geelonggallery.org.au

Left: The Hunt, by John Brack, courtesy Geelong Gallery
Above: The Pier Head, by Stanhope Forbes, courtesy Geelong Gallery

ARTS

PERFORMING ARTS

The **Geelong Performing Arts Centre** (tel 5225 1216), known universally as 'gee-pack', provides the community with a full range of modern, comfortable performance spaces. These are used by top-class touring companies and artists (there's an annual subscription season of theatre and dance) as well as by local theatre groups. Venues include the 800 seat proscenium arch Ford Theater, the studio-style Blakiston Theatre, and dance and rehearsal studios.

Deakin University opens the acoustically-superb **Costa Hall** (tel 5225 1216), in part of the old Dalgety's Wool Store, now the university's waterfront campus, to the public. This grand space now provides Geelong with a venue able to house large-scale concerts, seating up to 1500 patrons.

The Geelong Association of Music & Art is an umbrella organisation for the Music Society of Geelong, the Geelong Chorale, and the Geelong Repertory Society. The Geelong Repertory Society has its own small theatre, **The Woodbin**, in Coronation St, Geelong West.

There are a number of other significant performance venues, including the innovative **Courthouse** (tel 5227 0689), located in the former Geelong Law Courts and Police Station complex, which provides a dynamic world of arts based programs & events focused on young people aged from 12 to 25 years.

In Drysdale, the **Potato Shed** (tel 5251 1998) is a vibrant arts complex for the regional community. It also serves as a multi-purpose art and cultural centre for joint use by Bellarine Secondary College and the Catholic Regional College. The facility consists of a black box theatre seating 250, studios and practice rooms.

Left: Robert Bole, 13th Beach

Top: Natalie Russel, Torquay
Bottom: Robyn Alsop, Carnival

VISUAL ARTS

ARTHOUSE COLLECTIVE

The Arthouse Collective aims to nurture emerging artists, and to promote exhibitions, events and projects across all disciplines. The collective is run by artists for artists and is incorporated with Regional Arts Victoria.

BENNICKIM ART GALLERY

Bennickim displays an extensive and eclectic range of original artwork, ranging from sculptures to furniture to painting and photographs. The recently expanded gallery has new outdoor areas and great views.

Open: noon to 5 pm, Sat and Sun, or by appointment

Where: 215 Whites Rd, Mt Duneed (off Surfcoast Hwy)

Tel: 5264 1639

BRIM BRIM GALLERY

Located at Geelong Fine Arts School, there are regular openings and exhibitions by talented artists in a range of media and styles

Open: 11 am to 5 pm, Thu to Sun

Where: 560a La Trobe Blvd, Newtown

Tel: 5221 8874

BROUGHAM ART SCHOOL & GALLERY

This private art school and gallery provides a fully accredited Diploma of Arts, as well as a number of short courses. The gallery has a programme of high-quality contemporary exhibitions that change every three weeks.

Where: 1st floor, 73 Malop St

Tel: 5229 9984

www.broughamart.vic.edu.au

FRONT ART SPACE

Home of the Geelong Arts Alliance (see following), in partnership with the Geelong Performing Arts Centre, the space houses the Front Gallery, meeting and small workshop spaces.

Where: 79 Ryrie St

Tel: 5223 3242

GEELONG ARTS ALLIANCE

The Geelong Arts Alliance (tel 5223 3242, www.geelongartsalliance.org), is a cross-artform, membership-based organisation, committed to community cultural development in the Geelong region, collaborative actions by local practitioners, and the development and production of new contemporary art and ideas.

Top: Judy Scanlon, Winkipop
Bottom: Judy Scanlon, Winkipop
Right: Judy Scanlon, Winkipop

GEELONG ART SOCIETY

The Geelong Art Society (tel 5223 1825, www.geelongartsociety.com.au) is a community based non-profit organisation, and the largest regional art society in Victoria. Boasting a membership base of 229 artists, the society provides art classes for adults and children, as well as demonstrations, workshops and exhibitions. The society provides demon-strations within local state schools, and sponsors awards for children. It also provides free classes to handicapped people and subsidises art classes for abused children in the area. The Geelong Art Society operates from the Shearers Arms Gallery (see following), at 202 Aberdeen Street, Geelong West. It is a heritage classified building, which Geelong Art Society purchased and gave back to the community as a Visual Arts Centre; it is not a commercial entity.

GEELONG FINE ART SCHOOL

The Geelong Fine Art School was established in 1988 and is an artist-run school that provides a contemporary art education.

Where: 560 Latrobe Blvd

Tel: 5264 1523

GEELONG SCULPTORS

Formed in 2001 the Geelong Sculptors aim to promote the medium of sculpture through an annual exhibition and member networking.

Tel: 5221 6737

GORDON GALLERY

The Gordon Gallery (tel 5225 0533) is part of the Gordon Institute and aims to promote local artists through changing art and mixed media exhibitions, fashion parades and small concerts and recitals. It is a beautiful space in part of the Gordon's old building.

Where: 2 Fenwick St

Tel: 5225 0533

KARINGALLERY

Karingallery offers support and a quality exhibition space to people with disabilities. The gallery has monthly exhibitions and specializes in printed and 3D work.

Open: 10 am to 3 pm, weekdays

Where: 4 James St

Tel: 5221 1789

LITTLE MALOP GALLERY

The Little Malop Gallery (tel 5221 6505) is a vibrant art space presenting fine contemporary Australian art, five minutes walk from the waterfront. As well as diverse and changing exhibitions, the gallery maintains a program of feature exhibitions, presenting new work by gallery artists. Director Robert Avitabile is responsible for curating exhibitions.

Open: 10.30 am to 5.30 pm, Mon to Fri; 10.30 am to 4 pm Sat

Where: 101 Little Malop Street

Tel: 5221 6505

www.littlemalopgallery.com.au

Top: Judy Scanlon, Winkipop
Bottom: Judy Scanlon, Bells Beach

NARANA CREATIONS

Narana Creations welcomes visitors into an Aboriginal place. The gallery/ retail area displays a wide range of Aboriginal arts and crafts and the staff has extensive knowledge of history and culture. The art includes a variety of authentic printed panels, hand painted canvases, didgeridoos, boomerangs, clap sticks and many other items. In addition there's an extensive range of books, food and clothing.

Open: 9 am to 5 pm, Mon to Fri; 10 am to 4 pm, Sat

Where: 410 Torquay Rd, Grovedale

Tel: 5241 5700

www.narana.com.au

RYRIE ST ART GALLERY

The Ryrie St Art Gallery offers an exhibition space, an interesting range of art works, and framing services.

Where: 64 Ryrie St

Tel: 5229 7805

SEAVIEW GALLERY

Six rooms featuring Japanese furniture and outstanding works by over 40 Australian artists, including glass, jewellery, sculptures and paintings.

Open: 10.30 am to 5.30 pm, daily

Where: 86 Hesse St, Queenscliff

Tel: 5258 3645

SHEARERS ARMS GALLERY

The home of the Geelong Art Society, and formerly the Shearers Arms Hotel, this historic building, constructed in 1847, pre-dates the Gold Rush. Original artworks by local artists are displayed; exhibitions change frequently and admission is free.

Open: 11.00 am to 5.00 pm, daily

Where: 202 Aberdeen St, Geelong West

Tel: 5223 1825

TWINSILVER FINE ART GALLERY

Twinsilver exclusively represents the work of the Moongate and Blue Room studios. Moongate Studio is home to the modern, lyrical painting of Jan Francis, and the stone and metal sculptures by Geo Francis. Blue Room Studio is home to the metal sculptures of local flora and fauna created by Cinnamon James.

Where: 24 Wattlehill Grove, St Leonards

Tel: 5257 2177

WATHAURONG GLASS

Wathaurong Glass was formed to express aboriginal art in glass; this may include the use of kiln forming, sandblasting or any other technique the artist feels is suitable. Great pride is taken in producing unique artwork and high quality glass products, currently including partitions, windows, doors, splashbacks, platters, bowls and tabletops. All staff are Aboriginal and the company is structured so that the community of Wathaurong will be the beneficiaries of any profit.

Where: 62 Morgan St, North Geelong

Tel: 5277 0044

WINE

The story of Geelong's wine industry has two distinct chapters. The first chapter began in 1842 and was encouraged by Governor Charles La Trobe. La Trobe's wife came from Switzerland's Neuchatel wine-making region and this connection led to migration to the Geelong region by families with wine-making skills.

The first vines were planted at Pollock's Ford by David Pettavel and F. Brequet and by John Belperroud in the Barrabool Hills in 1842; they were soon followed by eleven new settlers from Neuchatel who planted vines around their homes in the Barrabool Hills, and in the late 1840s by German immigrants who settled at Germantown (now Grovedale).

By the late 1870's around 400ha were planted with vines and there were 116 vineyards, making Geelong Victoria's largest wine-making district. The district specialized in Australia's premier table wines, when most other regions (especially those in warm regions like the Barossa and north east Victoria) produced fortified, sweet wines much like the wines that today are often called 'stickies'.

Wineries from Geelong won a number of prestigious international awards, but disaster was waiting in the wings. The catalyst was a tiny aphid, known as Phylloxera, that attacks the roots of the vines, and progressively reduces yield. Phylloxera's first appearance in Australia was at Fyansford in 1877. The Government ordered the immediate destruction of infested vineyards, and a number of factors, including the economic depression of the 1890s, and the fashionable preference for sweet wines, meant that the vineyards were not replanted.

The fact that Geelong had once been internationally famous for its wines was forgotten by most people - but not all. Dr Daryl Sefton, a veterinary surgeon, and the great-grandson of two of the early Swiss migrants, grew up hearing stories of Geelong's wine era. He and his wife Nini set out to start the second chapter of Geelong's wine story and established Idyll vineyard at Moorabool in 1966 with phylloxera resistant stock. In 1983 the story came full circle when the Idyll Cabernet Shiraz won a gold medal at the Brussels Mondiale Selection – Geelong's first international gold award this century. In 1999 Idyll was bought by Vince and David Littore and became part of their Jindalee Estate.

The same ingredients that led to the success of the Geelong region in the 1860s the soils and climate still existed and other pioneers followed the Sefton's lead, including Tom Maltby at Mt Anakie; Stuart Hooper with winemaker Garry Farr at Bannockburn; Alister Scott at Tarcoola, Lethbridge; Ken Campbell at Mt Duneed; and Bruce Hyett at Prince Albert, Waurn Ponds.

Today, the level of plantings, at around 400 ha, is around the same as it was in the 1870's. There are now more than 40 vineyards, many of which are open for cellar-door tastings and sales; a number of which have excellent restaurants, and a few that have accommodation as well.

Left: Joe Mortelliti, Spray Farm

There are four distinct regions within the Geelong area - the Bellarine Peninsula, Moorabool Valley, Waurn Ponds and Anakie - each producing distinctive styles reflecting climatic and soil influences. Soil types vary from sandy loams, to red soils over limestone, to heavy black volcanic soils, and the microclimates vary from exposed maritime conditions on the peninsula to sheltered valley floors in the Moorabool Valley. The cool climate, hand pruning and picking, and low yields are producing complex strongly-characteristic wines.

AMIETTA VINEYARD & WINERY

Amietta is on a north facing slope of the Moorabool Valley and uses organic viticultural methods. Winemaking is based on traditional European methods; the riesling is cool fermented in closed tanks while the cabernet-merlot is fermented in small open vats.

Cellar Door: By appointment

Where: 30 Steddy Road (off Smith Road), Lethbridge

Tel: 5281 7407

ANAKIE RIDGE VINEYARD & RESTAURANT

Anakie Ridge was planted in 1998, and aims for organic methods wherever possible. The winemaking tends towards the traditional, using small vat fermentation, minimum oaking and filtration to bring out the complexity of the fruit. The restaurant offers honest, hearty Italian food, and million dollar views.

Cellar Door & Restaurant: 11 am to 5 pm, weekends

Where: 2290 Ballan Road, Anakie

Tel: 5284 1214

AUSTIN'S BARRABOOL WINES

Pamela and Richard Austin established Austin's Barrabool Wines in 1982 as a small family business on land that was recognised more than 140 years ago as ideal wine producing country. Today, Austin's Barrabool Wines has vineyards in Waurn Ponds and Sutherlands Creek.

Cellar Door: By appointment

Where: 50 Lemins Rd, Waurn Ponds

Tel: 5241 8114

BARWON PLAINS WINERY

Barwon Plains offers a selection of pinot noir, shiraz and chardonnay. The winery achieved recognition for its shiraz, winning the Gold Medal at the 2002 Geelong Show.

Cellar Door: 11 am to 5 pm, Wed and weekends, or by appointment

Where: 61 Trebeck Court, Winchelsea

Tel: 5267 2792

Left: Bruce Kirby, Vines
Above: Artist Photographer, Vines

BELLARINE ESTATE & RESTAURANT

Bellarine Estate was established in 1996 to grow and produce fine Australian boutique wines. Often produced in very small quantities, the wines aspire to intense flavours, colour and cellaring potential; they include sauvignon blanc, chardonnay, viognier, pinot noir, shiraz and merlot. The wine, along with excellent seafood and Tuscan-style fare is available from a restaurant which is housed in a renovated 1920's farmhouse. The property has spectacular views of the bay.

Cellar Door & Restaurant: 11 am to 5 pm daily; lunch daily; dinner Fri and Sat

Where: 2270 Portarlington Road, Bellarine

Tel: 5259 3310

BELLBRAE ESTATE – LONGBOARD WINES

Longboard Wines aim to reflect a relaxed coastal lifestyle. Nestled in the valley of Spring Creek, the vineyards trap the warmth and shelter needed for optimum ripening over summer. Wines include sauvignon blanc/semillon, chardonnay, pinot noir and shiraz.

Cellar Door: 10.30 am to 5 pm, Fri to Sun

Where: 520 Great Ocean Road, Bellbrae

Tel: 5264 8480

www.bellbraeestate.com.au

CLYDE PARK

Clyde Park overlooks the Moorabool River, 30 km north of Geelong. The property was established in 1981. There are now thirty-five acres under vine, expanding the existing pinot noir and chardonnay, with shiraz, sauvignon blanc and pinot gris. The soil varies from silt/clay to sand loam with basalt over a limestone base. Plantings on our north-easterly slopes provide maximum exposure to sunlight, while the river flat area offers warmth and wind protection.

Cellar Door: 11.00 am to 4.00 pm, weekends and public holidays

Where: 2490 Midland Highway, Bannockburn

Tel: 5281 7274

www.clydepark.com.au

COATSWORTH WINES

Where: 145 Coatsworth Rd, Portarlington

Tel: 0409 429 608

CURLEWIS WINERY

Curlewis is on the Bellarine Peninsula. Owners Rainer Breit and Wendy Oliver are committed to producing premium cool-climate wines. All wines are made by hand using traditional French methods. The vineyard consists of 1.6 hectares of 17 year old pinot noir vines in black cracking clay over limestone marl.

Cellar Door: By appointment

Where: 55 Navarre Road, Curlewis

Tel: 5250 4567

Left: Joe Mortelliti, Lake Connewarre

DEL RIOS WINERY

Del Rios is a family-owned winery on the western slopes of Mt Anakie, on 14 hectares of rich, black volcanic and grey alluvial soil with a granitic sand base. The property rises to a high plateau with views over Corio Bay, the You Yangs and Geelong. The adventurous can climb to the top of Mt Anakie, a 2km walk, for views of Melbourne. You might be accompanied of a pair of wedge-tail eagles that soar above the vineyard. All vines are hand pruned and hand harvested.

Cellar Door: 11.00am to 4pm, weekends

Where: 2320 Ballan Road, Anakie

Tel: 5284 1221

www.delrios.com.au

DONAGHADEE VINEYARDS

Where: 65 Burrows Rd, Lethbridge

Tel: 5281 7364

INNISFAIL VINEYARDS

Innisfail Homestead was built during the gold rush years as an overnight stop for people as they headed for the Ballarat goldfields. It's in the picturesque Moorabool Valley at Batesford, 10km from Geelong. The vines sweep up terraced hills from the river flats on rich black soil over layers of limestone. Innisfail Vineyard was re-established in 1980 with plantings of cabernet sauvignon, chardonnay and rhine riesling and later addition of pinot noir and merlot.

Cellar Door: By appointment

Where: Cross Street, Batesford

Tel: 5276 1258

JINDALEE ESTATE

With magnificent views of the beautiful Moorabool Valley, Jindalee Estate (formerly Idyll Wines) is Geelong's oldest vineyard, planted in 1966. Fettlers Rest wines are made on the estate from old vines: shiraz, cabernet/shiraz, pinot noir, chardonnay and gewurztraminer. Jindalee Wines from vineyards on the Murray River, near Mildura are also available for tasting. Tastings are free, and there are plenty of wines to choose from, including bargain cleanskins.

Cellar Door: 10.00 am to 5.00 pm, daily

Where: 256 Ballan Road, Moorabool

Tel: 5276 1280

www.jindaleewines.com.au

STAUGHTON VALE VINEYARD & WINERY

Staughton Vale Vineyard, in the Anakie Hills north of Geelong, offers sales and tastings of a range of handcrafted boutique wines. Staughton Cottage incorporates cellar door sales and a restaurant that offers fine dining every weekend. Luxury bed and breakfast accommodation is also available.

Cellar Door & Restaurant:

10am-5pm Friday, Saturday, Sunday and Monday

Cnr Ballan & Staughton Vale Rd, Anakie

Tel: 5284 1477 **Email:** staughtonvalewines@bigpond.com

Left: Joe Mortelliti, Scotchmans Hill

KILGOUR ESTATE WINERY & RESTAURANT

Established in 1989 Kilgour Estate creates fruit-driven pinot noirs, chardonnay and cabernet sauvignons. There are great views as well as high-quality gourmet food, specializing in local seafood. There's also a renovated cottage that accommodates two couples.

Cellar Door & Restaurant: 10 am to 5 pm seven days; lunch Wed to Sun; dinner Sat

Where: 85 McAdams Lane, Bellarine

Tel: 5251 2223

LETHBRIDGE WINES

Lethbridge Wines was founded in 1996 by three friends who believe in the importance of soil, climate, aspect and bio-diversity in the production of distinctive wines. Organic principles and traditional winemaking processes are followed. Varieties include merlot, pinot noir, viognier, zinfandel, sangiovese, brunello and chardonnay.

Cellar Door: 10 am to 5 pm, weekends

Where: 74 Burrows Rd

Tel: 5281 7221

www.lethbridgewines.com

LEURA PARK ESTATE

Leura Park Estate began in 1995 with an initial 20 acre planting of Chardonnay. The gently undulating vineyard faces north with views across Corio Bay to the You Yangs. With a cool, maritime climate Leura Park experiences a long cool-to-mild growing season. Soils are sandy loam over clay. Leura Park also provides snacks and coffee by the fire in winter or on the terrace in warmer weather.

Cellar Door: Open 11 am to 6 pm, Fri to Sun; Christmas and Easter open daily

Where: 1400 Portarlington Road, Curlewis via Drysdale

Tel: 5253 3180

MT ANAKIE WINERY & RESTAURANT

Established in 1967, on the northern slope of Mt Anakie, the vineyard has great views. It grows biancone, chardonnay, riesling, semillon, cabernet and shiraz, as well as producing a tawny port, lexia and a sweet rose. Owner, Austrian born Otto Zambelli, also caters for group functions - they will even pick up and return you home by bus! Dine in rustic Austrian style overlooking a herd of red deer and emus.

Cellar Door: 11 am to 5 pm, daily

Where: 130 Staughton Vale Rd,

Tel: 5284 1256

MT DUNEED WINERY

Established in 1969 by Ken Campbell, Mt Duneed produces a range of sparkling, table and fortified wines.

Cellar Door: 11 am to 5 pm, weekends, or by appointment.

Where: 70 Feehan's Road, Mount Duneed.

Tel: 5264 1281

Left: Robert Bole, Torquay
Above: Artist Photographer, Pettavel vines

McGLASHAN'S WALLINGTON ESTATE

Cellar Door: By appointment

Where: 225 Swan Bay Rd, Wallington

Tel: 5250 5760

MERMERUS VINEYARD

Classic cool climate chardonnay and pinot noir made with traditional methods.

Cellar Door: 1st Sunday of every month

Where: 60 Soho Rd, Drysdale

Tel: 5253 2718

PETTAVEL WINERY & RESTAURANT

The impressive modern winery and restaurant overlook the rolling hills of Waurn Ponds and rows of shiraz. Facilities include a glass walled terrace dining area seating up to 160 guests and a boardroom suitable for private functions and corporate events. The outstanding restaurant is open seven days a week for lunch, serving the best local ingredients; flavours are fresh, vibrant and unique. Wine tasting, sales and light tasting platters are available from the cellar door.

Cellar Door & Restaurant: 10:30am - 5:30pm daily Lunch daily. Facilities for private functions, weddings and corporate events.

Where: 65 Pettavel Road (Off Princes Highway), Waurn Ponds

Tel: 5266 1120

www.pettavel.com

POLLOCKSFORD VINEYARDS

Varieties are pinot noir, shiraz and chenin blanc.

Cellar Door: By appointment

Where: 335 Pollocksford Rd

Tel: 0419 888 700

THE MINYA VINEYARD & WINERY

The Minya Winery is between Torquay and Barwon Heads off Blackgate Rd. Established in 1974, within salt spray distance of the ocean, the varieties that have thrived are cabernet sauvignon, shiraz, merlot, grenache, chardonnay and gewürztraminer. Light meals are served in the peaceful surroundings overlooking Bream Creek. There is also cabin accommodation and, from January to April, an outdoor concert series.

Cellar Door: every weekend from Christmas to Easter

Where: Minya Lane, Connewarre

Tel: 5264 1397

MT ANAKIE WINERY

Mt Anakie Winery produces high-quality wines from some of the oldest vines in the district – and there's a tawny port as well. A rustic Austrian-style atmosphere, a lovely valley, great views, a private zoo, plus a restaurant mean that Mt Anakie Winery is a great place to visit. The restaurant caters for functions from 20 to 80 people (bookings essential).

Cellar door open 7 days a week 11am-5pm.

Functions catered for 20-80 people. Bookings essential.

130 Staughton Vale Rd. Anakie 3221

Tel: (03) 5284 1256 **Fax:** 52 841405

Left: Robert Bole, Western Beach

PRINCE ALBERT VINEYARD

Prince Albert was the first vineyard to be reestablished in the Waurn Ponds valley, one of the early centres for Geelong winemaking. On the site of the original Prince Albert Vineyard, Bruce Hyett, recognizing conditions that are similar to those that produce the great French burgundies, planted only pinot noir, which was rare in those early days. The first vintage was in 1978 and many outstanding pinots have been produced over the years, using organic viticultural methods.

Cellar Door: By appointment

Where: 92 Lemins Rd, Waurn Ponds

Tel: 5241 8091

PROVENANCE WINES

Provenance Wines was established in 1997 to make premium wines for a select group of growers from the Geelong region. All Provenance wines are single vineyard wines, crop levels are kept to a minimum and only fruit displaying a profound depth of flavour is used in the production of the wines. A combination of old-world techniques and the most advanced technology is utilised.

Cellar Door: By appointment

Where: Pollocksford Rd, Barrabool

Tel: 5272 2362

www.provenancewines.com.au

RIVER MOORABOOL ESTATE

Where: 226 Robertsons Rd, Lethbridge

Tel: 5281 7102

ST REGIS VINEYARD

St Regis has shiraz vines growing on a trellis system at Waurn Ponds, on the corner of Anglesea Rd and the Princes Hwy, on north facing limestone based, rich red-brown soil.

Where: 35 Princes Hwy, Waurn Ponds

Tel: 5241 8406

SCOTCHMANS HILL VINEYARD & WINERY

Scotchman's Hill is a high quality vineyard that has done a great deal to lift the profile of the Bellarine Peninsula; its wines rarely disappoint. The pinot noir is full of ripe fruit and the sauvignon blanc is always delicious. At the cellar door you can also taste the wines from the Browne family's other label, Swan Bay.

Cellar Door: 10.30 am to 4.30 pm daily

Where: 190 Scotchmans Rd, Drysdale

Tel: 5251 3176

www.scotchmanshill.com.au

Left: Robert Bole, St Leonards
Above left: Artist Photographer, Pettavel Restaurant
Above right: Artist Photographer, Pettavel Winery

SHADOWFAX WINERY & RESTAURANT

Brilliant contemporary architecture near Werribee Park, and state-of-the-art winemaking. Shadowfax makes wines from its vineyards in a number of Victoria's wine-making regions, including two pinot noir vineyards near Geelong (at Darriwill near Bannockburn, and at Swan Bay).

Cellar Door & Restaurant: 11 to 5 pm daily;
lunch weekends and public holidays

Where: K Road, Werribee

Tel: 9731 4420

www.shadowfax.com.au

TARCOOLA ESTATE

Where: Spillers Rd, Lethbridge

Tel: 5281 9245

SPRAY FARM

The fully restored historic homestead and gardens of Spray Farm, built in 1851, offers a magnificent venue for events, conferences, functions and weddings. With expansive water frontage, the property boasts spectacular views of the You Yangs, Port Phillip Bay and Melbourne. The property was bought by the Browne family of Scotchmans Hill in 1994 and a major restoration process has returned it to former glory. It is now home to the Spray Farm Summer Festival and Audi Spray Farm International One Day Horse Trials. The unique cellar door is in the restored stables of the historic homestead and offers tastings of all current Scotchmans Hill Group wines. The wine bar café offers a changing selection of light food featuring fine regional produce and an extensive cellar of local and international wines.

House: open daily

Cellar Door: 10.30 am to 4.30 pm, weekends and public holidays

Where: 2275 Portarlington Road, Portarlington

Tel: 5251 3176

www.sprayfarm.com.au

STAUGHTON VALE VINEYARD & RESTAURANT

Established in 1986 and producing cabernet sauvignon, merlot, cabernet franc, malbec, petit verdot, riesling, semillon, chardonnay and pinot noir. Vines were first planted in 1986, and Paul Chambers is one of the original winemakers in the region. His wines have won has won numerous awards. In addition to great wines, there is an attractive cottage restaurant that serves an innovative lunch menu, morning and afternoon teas. Luxury bed and breakfast accommodation is also available.

Cellar Door & Restaurant: 10am-5pm Friday, Saturday, Sunday and Monday

Where: Cnr Ballan & Staughton Vale Rd, Anakie

Tel: 5284 1477

Left: Robert Bole, Swan Bay
Above: Joe Mortelliti, Ceres

WAYBOURNE VINEYARD

Waybourne Vineyard is on the north-facing slopes of the Waurn Ponds valley, an area that was favoured by Geelong's original vignerons. The vineyard was re-established in 1980. The grapes are hand picked and traditional methods are used in crushing and pressing the grapes.

Cellar Door: 11 am to 5 pm Sat, Sun and school holidays

Where: 60 Lemins Rd, Waurn Ponds

Tel: 5241 8477

WOLSELEY WINES

Wolseley Wines lie on the gently sloping hills, with gravelly ironstone soils, just off the Great Ocean Road. There are plantings of pinot noir, cabernet sauvignon, shiraz, cabernet franc, chardonnay and semillon. The grapes are hand picked and there is an emphasis on traditional processes.

Cellar Door: Great Ocean Road Wine Centre (tel

Where: 1790 Hendy Main Road, Paraparap

Tel: 0412 990 638

ZEST

Zest serves meals from a contemporary a la carte menu Wed to Sat nights, and $10 lunch specials (including a glass of wine, soft drink or coffee) from Mon to Fri. There's a monthly wine appreciation night with a set menu and complementing wines. For special occasions there's a private function room. Zest can cater to almost anything you desire... which is why Zest does it Best! Your hosts Paul and Anita Wowk.

188 Moorabool Street. Geelong 3220

Tel: (03) 5229 1388 **Fax:** [03] 5229 0933

Left: Robert Bole, Point Impossible

Top: Joe Mortelliti, Portarlington
Bottom: Artist Photographer, Waterfront

FOOD

Close to the ocean and to the Western District – Geelong and the Peninsula are perfectly positioned to take advantage of the growing number of high-quality, regional specialties being produced. Sheep cheeses from Meredith, fresh crayfish flown into Barwon Heads from King Island, Angel Cardoso's hams and salamis, Portarlington mussels, sourdough bread and ice-cream from Irrewarra, Screaming Seed's spices from Bellbrae, and strawberries from Wallington are just some of the gourmet products that Geelong shops now stock.

Good places to find interesting local products include **Warren & Hutch**, the **Newtown Provedore**, and **V&R Vegetable Fruit & Vegetable Market** all on Pakington St. And while you're on Pakington St, it's worth visiting three excellent bottle shops, all with good stocks of local wines: **Bannockburn Cellars**, **Wine Justice** and at the river end, **Randall's The Wine Merchant**. The **Geelong Farmer's Market** is a showcase for the region's produce and is held in Little Malop Street, every second Saturday each month, from 9.00 am to 2.00 pm.

The (relatively recent) days when eating out meant either a roast at the Carlton Hotel's Carvery, or fried rice in the Tien Wah Café across the road are – thankfully – long gone. Restaurateurs have had to overcome competitive pressure from Melbourne's brilliant restaurants, which are only an hour down the road, but increasingly they're holding their own.

A number of restaurants and pubs in central Geelong, and a number of winery and beachside restaurants, now offer outstanding eating experiences. Geelong's cappuccino culture has also started to gather steam. The waterfront and Pakington St are at last providing places where the joys of reading a newspaper, watching the world go and sipping a good coffee can be combined.

There are a number of acclaimed restaurants scattered around the inner city:

- **2 Faces**, on Malop St, located in an 1857 bank has a well-deserved reputation for creative excellence
- **Bamboleo** on Little Malop St presents authentic Andalusian cooking
- **Bazil's**, on Cunningham St, is a bit hard to find, but worth it for high-quality Mediterranean-inspired cooking; **Bazil's Too** in Barrabool Rd, Highton is a welcome addition to the scene
- **Café Brulee**, on Pakington St, is a basic-looking café – but with fantastic food
- **Empire Grill**, on McKillop St, is a consistently excellent restaurant with a 'serious' menu - a favourite with locals
- **Giuseppe's Café** on Pakington St is famous for robust, high-quality Italian cooking
- **Irrewarra Bakery** on James St is a great place for simple but delicious lunches, not to mention excellent bread and coffee
- **Le Parisien** is an institution, now with a bayside location
- **l'espresso** on Ryrie St is a stylish café-style lunch place
- **Sailors Rest**, at the waterfront end of Moorabool St, has an Italian-inspired menu
- **Warung Bali**, on Shannon Ave, is a small place with fresh and authentic Balinese cuisine
- **Zest**, on Moorabool St, is a newcomer with an interesting menu and a bit of style

Top: Artist Photographer, Sailors Rest
Bottom: Robyn Alsop, Potato picking, Bellarine

There are also a number of pubs with restaurant-quality dining rooms; three worth looking for are:

- **Cremorne Hotel** in Pakington St
- **Sawyers Arms** in Noble St
- **Scottish Chiefs** in Corio St

Not far from Torquay in Bellbrae, **Bellbrae Harvest**, is a mud brick restaurant that features local seasonal produce and is tucked into a beautiful valley. Barwon Heads has a profusion of good restaurants; two favourites not to be missed are the **Starfish Bakery**, and **At the Heads**, overlooking the river mouth and proving that great views and food can go together. **Poach** in Ocean Grove is smart and stylish, with Asian influences. Point Lonsdale and Queenscliff are well endowed with high-quality restaurants, with **Mietta's** at the Queenscliff Hotel, the pioneer with a well-deserved reputation. **Harry's by the Sea** has a strong following too. **Katialo** in Portarlington presents excellent Greek-inspired cooking.

It's also hard to go past some of the winery restaurants: a combination of vines, beautiful views, local wines and great food is hard to beat. **Pettavels**, **Oakdene** (an outstanding newcomer near Ocean Grove), **Kilgour Estate**, **Mt Anakie**, **Spray Farm**, **Bellarine Estate**, **Anakie Ridge** and **Staughton Vale** are all worth trying. Some of them only open on weekends and it's worth booking ahead (see the **Wine** section for opening hours and contact details).

See the **Business Listings** section at the back of this book for an extensive directory of restaurants.

Top: Artist Photographer, North and Carousel
Bottom: Bruce Kirby, Eastern Beach

PLACES TO STAY

Geelong & the Bellarine Peninsula have accommodation choices that will suit everyone and every budget. The local Tourist Information Centres (see next section) are the best places to start enquiries; the knowledgeable local staff will quickly present the options that meet your criteria.

In Geelong, the options include:

- **Four Points by Sheraton**, brand new, overlooking the bay and the new waterfront developments
- the **Mercure**, eight storeys, with a commanding position overlooking the bay and city
- **The Haymarket**, a boutique, luxury hotel in a beautifully restored 1855 building in Moorabool St
- a number of motels have good locations around the bay, including the **Sundowner Motor Inn** and **Comfort Inn Eastern Sands**, whilst the **Admiralty Inn** on McKillop St is central and home to the **Empire Grill** restaurant
- a growing number of comfortable, central bed and breakfasts, including **Ardara House, Chipchase, Gatehouse on Ryrie** and **Pevensey House 1892**
- apartments, including the **Nireeda Apartments** and **Kardinia Geelong Apartments**
- backpackers accommodation, including the **National Hotel**
- caravan parks with camping and self-contained cabins, including the **Barwon Caravan & Tourist Park**, just 2 km from the city centre

The choices are even wider in the regions surrounding Geelong and on the Bellarine Peninsula. Each region and township has its own special character. Several wineries (see separate **Wine** section) and **Bellbrae Harvest** offer cabin accommodation. There are a range of heritage hotels and guesthouses at Queenscliff, and all the seaside towns offer great beachside camping grounds with cabins. Holiday houses are for rent all year round (contact local real estate agents) and are especially good value outside of school holidays. These days you can do much better than a dusty fibro shack!

On the Bellarine Peninsula, the options include:

- the luxurious **Ozone**, **Queenscliff** and **Vue Grand** hotels, with their excellent restaurants
- self-catering accommodation like the **Torquay 1903 Period Cottages** and the modern **Lonsdale Light Houses**
- **Bells Beach Lodge** in Torquay - for backpackers
- the wonderful camping ground at **Barwon Heads** (featuring Sea Change locations)

See the **Business Listings** section at the back of this book for an extensive directory of accommodation.

VISITOR INFORMATION CENTRES

The Visitor Information Centres in Geelong and on the Bellarine Peninsula are outstanding resources. Packed with free information, and staffed by knowledgeable locals, they can quickly advise on events, and local attractions. They are particularly helpful with questions about accommodation options.

GEELONG VISITOR INFORMATION CENTRE - NATIONAL WOOL MUSEUM

Located in the outstanding, historic National Wool Museum, right on the edge of the city centre, a short walk from the waterfront.

Where: Cnr Moorabool and Brougham Streets, Geelong

Tel: 1800 620 888 (Australian calls only); +61 3 5222 2900 (International)

www.greatoceanroad.org

gotvic@geelongcity.vic.gov.au

GEELONG & GREAT OCEAN ROAD VISITOR CENTRE

Located on the outskirts of Geelong, near the first outbreak of American fast-food stores.

Where: Stead Park, Princes Hwy, Corio

Tel: 1800 620 888 (Australian calls only); + 61 3 5275 5797 (International)

www.greatoceanroad.org

gotvic@geelongcity.vic.gov.au

MARKET SQUARE VISITOR INFORMATION CENTRE

Located in the central Market Square Shopping Centre, this is a relatively small kiosk at the Moorabool St entrance.

Where: Market Square, Moorabool St, Geelong

Tel: 5222 6126

TORQUAY VISITOR INFORMATION CENTRE

Located in the famous Surfworld Surfing Museum, with a great collection of souvenirs, in addition to comprehensive information.

Where: Beach Rd, Surf City Plaza, Torquay

Tel: 5261 4219

www.visitsurfcoast.com

torquayvic@iprimus.com.au

QUEENSCLIFF VISITOR INFORMATION CENTRE

An outstanding information centre; even locals will learn something!

Where: 55 Hesse Street, Queenscliff

Tel: 5258 4843 or freecall 1300 884 843

www.queenscliffe.vic.gov.au

info.centre@queenscliffe.vic.gov.au

Left: George Stawicki, North, Corio Bay

Top: George Stawicki, Geelong
Bottom: George Stawicki, Geelong

GEELONG

Geelong is Victoria's second largest city, but it's just 72 km, and less than an hour's travel time from Melbourne. Suburban sprawl seems to be rapidly closing the gap between the two. This proximity to Melbourne can work both for and against Geelong… On the other hand, the beaches of the Bellarine Peninsula and the Surf Coast are a 20 minute drive away. In this case proximity - to the coast - is only a positive!

In some ways Geelong is virtually a suburb of Melbourne; there are certainly Melbourne suburbs whose commuters have similar travelling times to those who travel from Geelong. Proximity means there is easy access to the best Melbourne can offer in terms of restaurants, sports, arts and entertainment, but proximity has sometimes made it hard for local venues to get going, and has sometimes left Geelong feeling somewhat unfairly overshadowed.

In reality, Geelong is less a suburb of Melbourne, and more a large country town on the coast - with the emphasis on country and coast. Its most natural point of comparison should not be with a vast metropolis, but with other proud regional cities. Wherever you stand, open paddocks are either visible, or less than a fifteen minute bike ride away, or both. Kids grow up thinking about beaches, not shopping centres.

The people of Geelong move to a different rather less urgent drum beat; they still seem to have time to talk; shop assistants are still genuinely friendly. The anonymity of a big city, which can be a blessing and a curse, doesn't hold up - if Americans talk about six degrees of separation, in Geelong it's three degrees of separation. People know each other and what is happening, they make connections, they notice.

Beyond the traffic in La Trobe Terrace Geelong is full of surprises. History has left a fascinating legacy – not always beautiful – but always interesting.

There's a gritty reality about the fabric of the city that reflects a culture of pragmatism and, at its best, innovation. Like a patched-up and improvised farmer's gate, Geelong buildings often have more than one life and the environment of Corio Bay has to work. Beauty often lies in the juxtaposition between the striking landscape, the wide skies, and the scale and ingenuity of industry.

The history of the City of Geelong is the history of European settlement in Victoria, and the city bears embellishments – and scars – from four economic phases.

The first boom in the 1850s was thanks to the Ballarat gold rush, when the harbour was a major gateway to the western goldfields. Then followed a long period where Geelong funnelled the riches of the Western District to the outside world, and built a string of world-famous woollen mills along the banks of the Barwon River. From the 1920's and particularly after WWII, Geelong developed as a major industrial centre and Corio Bay was gradually surrounded by industries.

Today, a fourth phase is unfolding. Geelong is still a manufacturing centre, but it is increasingly defined by tourism, education, surf, scientific research, a community of artists, and thriving service industries. Michael Kerr, of Jens Gaunt Real Estate, has noticed an increaing number of Melbournians moving to Geelong and he notes, "Geelong real estate has done very well in recent years, but by comparison to Melbourne it's still very good value."

The character of the city has always been defined by the bay: as a Wathaurong food bowl, as the landfall for prospectors, as the Western District's gateway, as an industrial harbour – and now as the centrepiece to a city that is increasingly focussed on 'lifestyle'.

Top: George Stawicki, Geelong
Bottom: George Stawicki, Geelong
Opposite left: Artist Photographer, Bay City Plaza
Opposite right: Robert Bole, Eastern Beach

WATERFRONT

Since Deakin University opened a campus in an abandoned wool store, Geelong has re-focused the waterfront as the natural place for kids to play, for fishermen to fish, and for everyone else to go for a walk, a coffee, a meal, or a swim. A number of significant developments have revitalised the entire stretch of coast from Drumcondra to Eastern Park. The shallow lagoon that is Corio Bay seems to be breathing once more, and the You Yangs imprint their ancient profile on the minds of all who stand, even briefly, on the shore.

CUSTOMS HOUSE & SAILORS' REST

One of the finest buildings in Geelong, the **Customs House** is a classically proportioned Georgian-style building, built in 1856 from locally quarried basalt rubble and sandstone cladding. The northern side backing on to the bay is three storeys, while its entry fronting Brougham St is only one storey. A small park with a water feature runs from the building to the Eastern Beach Rd, past the Sailors Rest Café and Restaurant. The Customs House is now occupied by Geelong Otway Tourism's administrative staff, but is not open to the public.

Sailors Rest is an interesting building in its own right. Completed in 1913, in honour of King Edward VII, Sailors Rest was designed to offer non-alcoholic (!) entertainment for sailors. It provided light snacks and activities like darts and billiards and dancing. The electric sign on the roof at the front of the building was erected in 1926 and was considered at the time to be the ultimate in technology. Today you don't have to be a sailor to enjoy the excellent food and coffee – and alcoholic beverages are sold!

EASTERN BEACH

Sea bathing at Eastern Beach has a history that goes back at least as far as 1844 when the first segregated baths were built. By the 1880s at least six sea baths, a hot sea bath and natural mineral springs operated along the beach front. Redevelopment of the area began in 1924 and it was gradually improved through to 1939. Eastern Beach is a unique art-deco inspired complex that was designed to make Geelong the ideal summer holiday destination! It is certainly a justifiably popular place for swimming and picnicking – particularly for families with young children.

WOOLSTORES

Across the road from the Customs House, and once lining both sides of Brougham St, are a number of massive woolstores that were, not so long ago, iconic Geelong names: Strachan, Dennys Lascelles, and Dalgety. The stores were built to store the Western District's golden fleece; wool bales would be brought into the Geelong stores, graded (classed), displayed for buyers (under natural light on the top floor), auctioned, and then dispatched around the world on the clippers lined up at the Cunningham and Yarra St piers.

Top: George Stawicki, Geelong
Bottom: Artist Photographer, Geelong Botanic Gardens
Opposite left: Artist Photographer, Geelong Botanic Gardens
Opposite right: Robert Bole, Geelong Botanic Gardens

GEELONG BOTANIC GARDENS

Daniel Bunce began planting the gardens in 1851, making Geelong the fourth oldest gardens in Australia. Bunce studied botany at the Kew Gardens in London, before accompanying Ludwig Leichardt on two expeditions as naturalist and botanist. One of his strongest interests was finding plants and birds that would adapt to Australian conditions; in addition to experimenting with plants he and the Geelong Acclimatisation Society bred blackbirds, thrushes and sparrows!

Thirty trees dating from these early days are now on the National Trust register of significant trees. Three of the most interesting are the Chinese **Gingko**, or **Maidenhair Tree** (planted in 1859), the **Chilean Wine Palm** (planted in 1869) and the bizarre **Cork Oak**. There are more 19th century features with shady lawn areas, hothouses and floral displays.

In 2002 a striking extension to the gardens was opened. It is in dramatic contrast to the original 19th century layout. Geelong has had a number of years of serious drought so one important design parameter was to feature plants that have evolved to live in arid environments. Local indigenous plants, especially from around the Brisbane Ranges, are featured, but there are also central Australian desert plants and a collection of succulents from southern Africa.

While most of the new section is young, some feature trees have been transplanted from within the gardens. These include the spectacular eight metre high **Grass Tree**, and a **Dragon Tree** that was originally planted by Daniel Bunce in 1851.

The oldest building in Victoria – the modest Customs House dating from 1838 – can also be seen tucked away at the back of the gardens. It looks very much like an unremarkable garden shed, which given the importance of sheds in subsequent Australian gardens, not to mention culture, seems appropriate.

The gardens are open from 7.30 am to 5 pm on weekdays, 7.30 am to 7 pm on weekends. Entry is free and the Friends of the Garden operate a small café in a shady corner.

Top: Artist Photographer, Carousel
Bottom: Artist Photographer, North, Cunningham Pier
Right: Artist Photographer, Carousel

THE CAROUSEL

The Geelong Carousel began life in bustling New York in 1892. At the turn of the century every carnival and circus worth its salt would have had a steam driven merry-go-round, but today less than 200 hand-carved wooden carousels survive. In its long life the Geelong Carousel must have given pleasure to countless children, and there is a particular magic seeing delighted children enjoying what seems – in 21st century terms – very innocent entertainment.

The complete history of the Carousel is unknown, but it was a mainstay at the Mordialloc Carnival from the 1920s to the 1950s. A used ticket butt from this period was found inside one of the horses during restoration. Restorers also found evidence that the Carousel went on the road as part of a travelling carnival.

The Carousel was finally dismantled and left in a paddock at Echuca before being auctioned and stored at Castlemaine. A vintage car restorer, Rick Furlong, heard of the existence of the Carousel, and despite having no prior knowledge of carousels, he was intrigued and decided to purchase it. It took two years of painstaking work to return the Carousel to its former glory. Forty layers of paint were scraped back to reveal the original colours. Each horse took 300 hours to restore. All but 12 of the 36 horses are original but the two chariots are replicas based on originals in America.

The Carousel, together with a restored steam engine and Gavioli Band Organ are housed in a glass pavilion designed by local architects McGlashan Everist.

The Carousel is open daily, 10.30 am to 5 pm, Monday to Friday; 10.30 am to 8 pm, Saturday; 10.30 am to 6 pm, Sundays. Entry to the pavilion is free; tickets for the ride are $2.50 for children, $3 for adults.

NORTH

North, an outstanding sculpture by Mark Stoner, sits on the edge of the Quay at the end of Moorabool St. Standing at the corner with Brougham St, the sculpture is framed by the trees at the south end of Moorabool St and can seem almost to float. The seven large pieces of the sculpture are ochre and grey, suggesting sails or fins, but they also connect with the ragged profile of the You Yangs on the other side of the bay.

BOLLARDS & BAY WALK

There is a pleasant bay walk from Limeburner's Point (where in 1847 Governor La Trobe found mysterious buried keys) to Rippleside Park. Along the way there are entertaining clusters of painted timber sculptures, or bollards, the work of local artist Jan Mitchell. They reflect local history and historical characters, and they seem to be breeding.

CUNNINGHAM PIER

Cunningham Pier is one of the most important Geelong piers, and is now the only one that survives from the 19th century. Once home to the fastest most beautiful sailing ships in the world, it now suffers the indignity of hosting a Smorgies all-u-can-eat restaurant. It is still used by the rare passenger vessels that call in, but its glory days were when ships like the Thermopylae, Lightning and Cutty Sark loaded wool then raced back to Britain in under 80 days.

MUSEUMS

NATIONAL WOOL MUSEUM

Wool has been an essential part of Australia's growth as a nation, and was the central plank to Geelong's development for the first 100 years. Geelong, more than any other city in Australia, has ridden on the sheep's back! The prospect of new grazing lands is what drove the early explorers and John Batman, and the first pastoralists, John Cowie and David Stead, arrived with a flock in March 1836. Geelong's commercial existence depended on the export of sheep products (from tallow to wool) and later on the processing of wool and the manufacture of woollen products.

In 1988, 152 years after the arrival of the first sheep, the National Wool Museum was established as Australia's only comprehensive museum of wool. The Museum is in an historic 1872 bluestone wool store not far from the waterfront.

The ground floor has changing exhibitions, souvenirs and sales of Australian -made wool and wool-related products. There's also a working example of a 1910 Axminster Carpet Loom which is operated by skilled carpet weavers. The loom uses the Jacquard punch card system to produce the National Wool Museum's own 'Manor House Rug'.

The first gallery focuses on the human effort, both past and present, involved in husbanding sheep and producing fleece. You can follow the path of the fleece through the stages of shearing, classing, wool pressing and dispatch to the world. Interactive displays offer the opportunity to taste what life in the shearing industry was like by walking through the recreated shearing quarters and watching sheep being shorn in the shearers shed.

Gallery Two offers an insight into the people and processes involved in the textile industry. The transformation of fleece to fabric is demonstrated by machinery actually used in the process. For many years, the rhythm of daily life for the thousands of mill workers in Geelong was determined by the sound of the mill whistles. You can sit in the kitchen of the mill worker's house and hear stories about the mill workers' lives.

Open: 9.30 am to 5 pm, daily
Admission: adult $7.50, concession $5.90, child $3.65, family $20
Where: Address: 26 Moorabool St, Geelong Victoria Australia
Tel: 5227 0701

Left: Joe Mortelliti, Ozone, Indented Head, Melbourne
Above: All Artist Photographer, National Wool Museum, except night shot, Robert Bole

Top: Artist Photographer, Ford Discovery Centre
Bottom: Artist Photographer, Ford Discovery Centre

FORD DISCOVERY CENTRE

After wool, came motor cars... Ford cars! The Ford Motor Company began assembly of Model T Fords, just across the road from the current location of the Ford Discovery Centre, in 1925. The Ford Discovery Centre is aimed at anyone who is interested in the past, present and future of motor cars – but will especially appeal to Ford fanatics.

It provides a unique behind-the-scenes opportunity to discover how cars are designed and built, but it also takes you through the Australian history of Ford. There is an impressive display of rare and historic cars, from the world-changing Model T, the first XK Falcon, Bathurst-winning Falcons and GTs, to the latest models hot off the production line. The Centre's most famous exhibit is a 1934 ute – the world's first utility vehicle, designed in Geelong by Lew Bandt.

There are also interactive displays (you can operate two assembly-line robots), a specially constructed mock design studio (including real clay models), crash-test dummies, special cutaway vehicles showing the inner workings of a car and a race simulator. You can also take a virtual 'factory tour' in the theatrette.

The Ford Discovery Centre is located in a historic wool store in the waterfront precinct, a short walk from the National Wool Museum and the bay.
Open: 10 am to 5 pm, daily except Tuesdays
Admission: adults $6, concession $4, child $3, family $15
Where: cnr Gheringhap and Brougham Sts
Tel: 5227 8700

OLD GEELONG GAOL

The Old Geelong Gaol was in use until 1991, but it is now a ghoulish tourist attraction. The gaol has remained virtually unchanged since it was built in stages from 1849 to 1864 out of local bluestone. Its design was based on Pentonville prison in England and construction was carried out by convicts who were kept in hulks on Corio Bay.

The prison gallows were first used in 1863 when James Murphy was hanged for beating a policeman to death with a hammer; a display depicts this event. Notorious inmates included the brutal bushranger Mad Dog Morgan, Edward Eastwood, the Faraday kidnapper, and Mark 'Chopper' Reed. Volunteer guides point out the steel plate reinforcement on the wall through which Eastwood and another prisoner tunneled to brief freedom.

The interior is, not surprisingly, bleak. A tour takes in the normal cells (some featuring interesting graffiti), the solitary confinement cells (unchanged since they were last used in 1991), workshops, exercise areas, and watchtowers.
Open: 11 am to 3 pm, Thu and Fri; 1 to 4 pm, Sat and Sun and school holidays
Where: cnr Myers and Swanston Sts
Tel: 5221 8292

MARITIME MUSEUM

Geelong's connection with the bay, and its maritime past is celebrated in a museum housed in the renovated stables of the historic Osborne House mansion, overlooking Corio Bay. The beautiful bluestone mansion was built for Robert Muirhead in 1858 and has been used as a private residence, a guest house, a hospital, Australia's first naval college (from 1913 to 1915), the base for Australia's submarine fleet, and as the Shire of Corio's offices. The Museum's displays include typical luggage of an early passenger, scaled models of ships that either visited Geelong or called the port home, and relics and memorabilia related to trade and navigation. There is an early 'fold out' canoe used for secret missions during WWII, and early diving equipment.

Open: 10 am to 4.30 pm, daily

Where: The Stables, Osborne House, Swinburne St, North Geelong

Tel: 5277 3808

NOTABLE BUILDINGS

BARWON GRANGE

Built in 1855, Barwon Grange is an elegant Gothic-style mansion overlooking the Barwon River. It was built for a successful businessman, Jonathan Porter O'Brien, and features steep gables, attic dormer windows, and wide verandahs. A fine collection of early Victorian objects and furniture has been gathered to match an authentic 'List of Contents' made in 1856 and is one of the most authentic and complete collections the trust owns.

Where: Fernleigh St (off Fyans St West)

Open: 11 am to 4.30 pm, Wed and Sun

Tel: 5221 3906

CHRIST CHURCH

Christ Church (Anglican) at the top of Moorabool St, designed by Edmund Blacket. Edmund Blacket arrived in Sydney in 1842 and was appointed Colonial Architect in 1849. He is best known for his church architecture and for his designs for the University of Sydney. Christ Church was built from 1843 to 1847 and is the state's oldest church in continuous use.

Where: cnr McKillop and Moorabool Sts

CUSTOMS HOUSE

One of the finest buildings in Geelong, the Customs House is a classically proportioned Georgian-style building, built in 1856 from locally quarried basalt rubble and sandstone cladding. The northern side backing on to the bay is three storeys, while its entry fronting Brougham St is only one storey. A small park with a water feature runs from the building to the Esplanade, past the Sailors Rest Café and Restaurant. The Customs House is now occupied by Geelong Otway Tourism's administrative staff, but is not open to the public

Where: cnr Brougham and Moorabool Sts

Left: Joe Mortelliti, Barrabool Hills
Above: Artist Photographer, Customs House

Top: Robert Bole, St Mary of the Angels
Bottom: Bruce Kirby, St Mary of the Angels
Opposite left: Artist Photographer, Corio Villa
Opposite right: Artist Photographer, St Mary of the Angels

CORIO VILLA

Although there is ample evidence local artisans and tradesmen had superb skills, some wealthy home builders preferred to buy houses that were prefabricated in Europe. One of the most striking of these prefabricated buildings is Corio Villa, indeed it's considered to be one of the finest in Australia. It occupies a prime site overlooking Eastern Beach and is famous for its elaborate cast iron filigree.

Corio Villa was prefabricated in Edinburgh in 1854 on behalf of Mr William Gray, a Crown Lands commissioner for the Portland district, but he died before the parts arrived in Geelong. Another Geelong businessman and the eventual owner of the Geelong Advertiser, Alfred Douglass, bought the house components at a sale price. Despite not having any plans, the house was successfully pieced together in 1856. The Douglass family lived in it until 1938, and it's still privately owned.

Where: cnr Fitzroy St and Eastern Beach Rd

MERCHISTON HALL

Merchiston Hall is a two storied Classical Revival mansion that was built for James Cowie, an early member of the Victorian Legislative Council, a pioneer saddler, and one-time mayor. The architects were Backhouse and Reynolds who designed many Geelong buildings including the Flinders National School (1858) Geelong Grammar School (1857) and the Church of Christ (1859). The building is privately owned, and is classified 'A' by the National Trust.

Where: 2A Garden St

ST MARY OF THE ANGELS

Whichever road you enter Geelong, the profile of the city is dominated by the fine profile of this majestic Catholic basilica, crowning the highest hill. If a single building was to stand as a Geelong icon, this would have to be the one.

In 1852 the architects Dowden and Ross drew up plans for a magnificent cathedral-like building, 200 feet long, 130 feet wide and costing 40,000 pounds. It was to feature a giant bluestone steeple and an exquisite rose window. Work commenced in 1854 but, perhaps because the parish took to the goldfields, work ceased in 1856. Construction did not commence again until 1871 and the church was finally dedicated in 1872 – despite the fact that the western steeple and two eastern spires were not installed. In 1931 work began on the completion of the church as it appeared in the original plans. Finally, in June 1937, the work was completed and St Mary of the Angels took full command of her hill.

Recently a $1.6 million restoration programme was completed and in 2004 the church was recognized by Rome as a basilica, a term which means it has great architectural significance. There are only five churches in Australia that are considered basilica; two of these are in Melbourne; they are St Patrick's Cathedral and Our Lady of Victories in Camberwell.

Where: Yarra St

Top: George Stawicki, Geelong
Bottom: George Stawicki, Geelong
Opposite left: Artist Photographer, Bandstand, Johnston Park
Opposite right: Artist Photographer, Town Hall

THE HEIGHTS HOUSE & GARDEN

The Heights, like Corio Villa, is prefabricated. In this case the 14-room timber house was imported from Hamburg, Germany, in 1855 for Geelong businessman Charles Ibbotson. Other buildings, including stables, dovecote, water tower and timber outbuildings, were constructed on site. There have been many modifications and additions over the years, including an internal remodeling in the 1930s, but the exterior below the eaves is original. The home is set in 1.6 hectares of National Estate-registered gardens, regarded as a significant example of a large 19th century landscaped urban garden. The house contains a large collection of Georgian furniture.

Open: 11 am to 4.30 pm, Wed and Sun

Where: 140 Aphrasia St

Tel: 5221 3510

WINTERGARDEN

Originally constructed as a Congregational Church in 1854, the Wintergarden features classical lines and unusually tall windows that create a lofty, naturally-lighted space. Even by Geelong standards, the building has had an interesting career: in 1878 it became a drill hall; in 1907 it became home to the Bollington Hop Beer Company; in 1914 soft drinks were manufactured by Taits; in 1920 McClintocks made vinegar, drinks and jellies; and in 1949 Carew's Dry Cleaning took over.

This beautiful building is now a unique complex with books, boutique clothing, antiques, a large garden gallery with a range of sculptures, water features and furniture, and a café serving breakfast, lunch and afternoon tea.

Where: 51 McKillop St.

Other notable buildings include:

- the Town Hall, built in the Greek Revival style; corner Gheringhap and Little Malop Sts; built in stages from 1855
- Telegraph Office, another Georgian-style sandstone building; next to the old GPO, Ryrie St; built in 1858
- Geelong Gaol, built in 1852; open to the public
- The Hermitage, a grand sandstone home built for George Armytage; Pakington St; built in 1859
- Matthew Flinders Girls High School, old building built in 1856
- Geelong College, Talbot St, old building built in 1871
- Geelong Post Office, Ryrie St, built in 1891
- The Reformed Theological College in Maud St was Geelong Grammar School, built in 1858.
- Scottish Chiefs Hotel, in Corio St, built in 1848 and one of the 10 oldest licensed premises in the state

Top: George Stawicki, Torquay
Bottom: George Stawicki, Torquay
Opposite: Natalie Russel, Torquay

TORQUAY

Torquay stands at the entry to the surf coast, or to the Bellarine Peninsula, depending on whether you travel east or west. It faces Bass Strait, 21 km south of Geelong, and it has been defined by its brilliant location: close to Geelong, but even closer to great waves.

For many years Torquay was a modest holiday township notable for uninspiring fibro shacks, and a large temporary population of cheery campers who would arrive on Boxing Day and depart on the Australia Day weekend. Coffee definitely meant instant, and cuisine came wrapped in newspaper. Today Torquay is an energetic township with smart new housing developments that is known world-wide as the centre for an innovative surf industry. The Gilbert St shopping centre is jam-packed with coffee shops (coffee means latte) and places to eat (newspaper is what you read).

Torquay was originally occupied by the Mon-mart clan of the Wathaurong Aboriginal people. The Mon-mart clan land extended from Spring Creek, which runs through the centre of Torquay, to Lake Connewarre and the Barwon River. William Buckley (see separate section) was the first white resident of the region. He was an escaped convict who was rescued by the Mon-mart clan and who lived with them for 32 years - much of the time around Breamlea, five km to the east.

Robert Zeally took up land in the vicinity in 1851. Torquay was referred to as Jan Guck on one early map of the area, and Puebla in the 1882 Victorian Municipal Directory, but the first common name for the small township was Spring Creek, which flows through the town, marking the divide between today's Torquay and Jan Juc.

By the 1870s, nearby Geelong was already a large city and picnickers, campers and fishermen began to make regular excursions to Spring Creek. James Follett settled in the area in 1871, built a boarding house, a bathing house on the beach, and provided a wagonette service to and from Geelong. He built the Pioneer Coffee Palace soon after the first land sale in 1886. Follett, who must have been a redoubtable entrepreneur, came from Torquay, in Devon, England. As these things happen, in 1889 the Torquay Improvement Association was formed and in 1892 the name of the town was formally changed to Torquay.

Another early family has given their name to a number of local places: the Bell family farmed behind Bells Beach; their homestead, Addiscott, was at Bellbrae.

Torquay is eight km north-east of Bells Beach, and the entire coast between Torquay and Bells can be surfed. Surfing at Bells began in the late 1940s, but did not really take off until after 1956 when an International Surf Life Saving Carnival brought the famous Duke Kahanamoku and a Hawaiian team with revolutionary fiberglass Malibu boards to Torquay. Over the next few years a keen group of Torquay surfers starting surfing Bells on a regular basis.

Top: George Stawicki, Torquay
Bottom: George Stawicki, Torquay
Opposite: Robert Bole, Torquay

A growing number of young Australians fell in love with the sport, and following the short board revolution of 1967 a number of fanatics started surf-related businesses in garages and derelict shops around Torquay – hoping to make a living, but more importantly planning to do a lot of surfing.

Rip Curl started making surfboards and in 1970 began making the first primitive surfing wetsuits, the product that has been the backbone of the company ever since. Quiksilver started with a revolutionary new design for boardshorts and went on to produce sheepskin boots and a range of surf wear. Piping Hot started in 1975 with wetsuits and has also moved on to clothing. All three companies are now multinational icons, and there are others like Beach Crew, Gash, Rojo and Strapper, who are snapping at their heels.

The Rip Curl Pro at Bells Beach has become an annual pilgrimage for surfers every Easter. It's the world's longest running professional surfing event, with a history of innovation stretching back to 1961, when the first contest was held, and 1973, when Rip Curl first sponsored the event. It attracts massive crowds every Easter and holds a proud place in surfing folklore. The natural amphitheatre at Bells Beach makes for an atmosphere unmatched anywhere in the world.

In addition to having significant industry in its own right, Torquay has become a dormitory suburb to Geelong. The township has a substantial residential area, three camping and caravan parks, a shopping area, and the extraordinary Surfworld Plaza, which includes the greatest concentration of surf shops, and surf gear in the world, plus an excellent surf museum.

Torquay Front Beach is a wide sandy, sheltered beach that curves from Yellow Bluff towards Point Danger (see the separate section on the Point Danger Marine Sanctuary). A grassy reserve with tall Norfolk pines fringes the beach. The point protects the beach from most ocean swells, making it popular with families seeking calmer waters for swimming and paddling. It is also referred to as Cosy Corner. Further to the east, Fishermans Beach (or Fishos) is a favourite for beach and boat fishing.

Known as the Back Beach, the ocean-facing surf beach draws big crowds in summer, and can be unbearably crowded at high tide. The surf is not great, but the beach is a favourite with learners any time of the year. There are a number of breaks along the beach and off Rocky Point. Lifesavers patrol daily in peak holiday times.

JAN JUC

The suburb of Jan Juc (after the original Jan Guck) lies across Spring Creek and past the Torquay Golf Club. The residential area of Jan Juc began in the mid 1960s, and its growth quickened in the 1980s. The cliff-lined sandy beach is popular with swimmers and surfers. With its tidy shore break it's a good, though busy, beach on a small swell. Lifesavers patrol daily in peak holiday times.

Top: George Stawicki, Torquay
Bottom: George Stawicki, Bells Beach
Opposite: Artist Photographer, Surfworld Surfing Museum

SURFWORLD PLAZA

Surfworld Plaza is a shopping centre and a tourist attraction in one. Whether you're a fanatical surfer, whether the boards are bolted on to your roof, or whether you've got no intention of immersing yourself in Bass Strait, Surfworld will still fascinate. It is the largest conglomeration of surf shops and surf gear in the world.

And surf gear does not just mean boys, boards, wetsuits and wax. Surf gear means fashion! Surf gear means jeans, t-shirts, bikinis, watches, hats, jewellery... and yes, there are still some of the best handcrafted surfboards available. At one level it seems to make little sense to have such intense competition in such a relatively small spot, but obviously the combined pull of the big names means that even the new little names find scraps of business.

SURFWORLD SURFING MUSEUM

In addition to the surf shops there are a number of cafes, and the excellent Surfworld Museum. The museum goes beyond a narrow definition of surf and celebrates Australia's beach culture, including clothing and musical fashions. It has one of the most extensive displays in the world of historical surfing gear and memorabilia, including an extraordinary collection of surfboards dating back to 1915, and a Surfing Hall of Fame. The museum also includes a theatre that screens surf movies, a wave-making tank, a paddling machine to test fitness, a machine to test balance on a surf board, board-shaping demos.

Open: 9 am to 5 pm daily

Cost: $6.50 for adults and $4.50 for children and concessions

Where: Surfworld Plaza

Tel: 5261 4606.

TORQUAY VISITOR INFORMATION CENTRE

Located alongside the Surfworld Surfing Museum, the Torquay Visitor Information Centre has a great collection of souvenirs, in addition to comprehensive information.

Where: Beach Rd, Surf City Plaza, Torquay

Tel: 5261 4219

www.visitsurfcoast.com

torquayvic@iprimus.com.au

POINT IMPOSSIBLE & BREAMLEA

Point Impossible is the next point to the east of Torquay's Point Danger and it shelters Buckley's Bay at the mouth of Thompsons Creek (also known as Bream Creek). It is thought there may be aboriginal burials in the area.

Thompsons Creek runs through a wetland of salt marshes and reedy canals and widens before it enters Buckley's Bay, which was named after William Buckley, a convict who escaped and spent 32 years living with the local Mon-mart aboriginals. Buckley spent much of his time in this area, no doubt because it was particularly rich in food resources, and built a hut somewhere in the vicinity. A natural well is also named after him.

The creek, the inland swamps and the sea reefs were, and are, rich in shell fish, and they are still an important breeding ground for bream. The same resources that sustained the Mon-mart soon attracted European fishermen, and by the 1920s, there were huts at Breamlea. During the Great Depression, squatters built permanent huts and eked out a living as best they could, again relying on the bounty of the sea and land. Freehold land was finally subdivided for residential purposes in 1942. The resulting small township, scarcely more than three house blocks wide, has a single store which serves the small number of residents and the caravan park.

Bancoora Beach is accessed at the eastern end of the Breamlea township. It's a beautiful crescent beach about one km long, between basalt, rocky points and reefs, and backed by a ti-tree covered dune. The Bancoora Surf Life Saving Club patrols the beach in summer; there are rips from time to time and the beach deserves respect.

Left: Robert Bole, Breamlea
Above: George Stawicki, Breamlea

Top: George Stawicki, Barwon Heads
Bottom: George Stawicki, Barwon Heads
Opposite: George Stawicki, Barwon Heads

BARWON HEADS

The township of Barwon Heads has an outstanding position. There are commanding views of the coast from the Bluff (or Flinders Point) and the town features a combination of sheltered estuary waters and great ocean beaches.

The sandy estuary is ideal for paddling, fishing and boating. Inland from the ocean heads, it is lined with mangroves, and it then opens up into a vast wetland and lake system. On the ocean side, 13th Beach is a wonderful stretch of sand and reefs, with some often underrated, but top-quality waves, as well as a patrolled section in summer. Behind 13th Beach there are now two of Australia's finest golf courses, the traditional Barwon Heads Golf Club links, and the new Beach Course designed by Tony Cashmore and Nick Faldo.

Known to the Wathaurong as Kolo:oit, the Bluff at the mouth of the Barwon river, was an important meeting and camping area for thousands of years. The Wathaurong's bark shelters have been replaced by a picturesque football ground, caravans and prefabs, but it is still a great place to camp: sheltered and shady, with great fishing and a reef teeming with life.

In recognition of outstanding environmental qualities the Bluff is now a protected Marine Reserve and the estuary, Reedy Swamp and Lake Connewarre is a State Game Reserve that has been listed under the Ramsar Convention as a wetland of international significance.

Barwon Heads' beauty has been recognised over the years by film and television makers. 13th Beach featured in the apocalyptic film On the Beach (based on the book by Neville Shute) starring Ava Gardner, Gregory Peck, Fred Astaire and John Meillion. At the time, Ava's unforgettable (although disputed) quote, when asked what she thought of Melbourne, was that Melbourne was an entirely suitable place to film the end of the world! Certainly, if you stand on the Bluff and look into a south-westerly gale you are left in no doubt you are standing on the southern edge of a southern continent and there is nothing between you and Antarctica.

Barwon Heads' current prosperity (and stratospheric property values) is in part due to the interest created by the ABC's much-loved Sea Change series that starred Sigrid Thornton as Laura. Laura's cottage, in the Barwon Heads Caravan Park, is available for rent, and Diver Dan's House is now part of At the Heads café/restaurant, a rare exception to the rule that great views and great food do not go together.

Top: George Stawicki, Barwon Heads
Bottom: George Stawicki, Barwon Heads
Opposite: Robyn Alsop, Surf Carnival

The Connewarre region was first settled by the Vagg family in the 1840s. Because of its relatively easy accessibility, development began on the Ocean Grove side of the river around 1854. Settlement on the other side at Barwon Heads was delayed until 1875. Barwon Heads was initially a boating, fishing and shooting destination, with a coffee palace, later named the Mt Colite Hotel, on the site of the present hotel. In the 1930s there was a significant fleet of 30 boats fishing primarily for barracouta.

The bridge between Ocean Grove and Barwon Heads is the longest wooden bridge in Victoria, and was completed in 1927; prior to its construction an open boat ferried people across the river. Because the bridge was such a late development, Barwon Heads is historically considered the starting point for the Great Ocean Road. Howard Hitchcock, who is credited as the founder of the Great Ocean Road, originally conceived of a coastal road stretching from Barwon Heads to Warrnambool; he went on to head the trust that was founded in 1918 to fund the road's construction.

JIRRAHLINGA KOALA & WILDLIFE SANCTUARY

The Jirrahlinga Koala and Wildlife Sanctuary is on three hectares of land a few minutes drive north of Barwon Heads. After many years of caring for orphaned and injured animals and birds, Tehree and Hamish Gordon have developed an outstanding privately-owned wildlife sanctuary. Tehree was recently awarded the title of 2004 Senior Australian of the Year.

Injured and orphaned birds and animals are brought in by government officers from various departments, as well as members of the public. The sanctuary and hospital can accommodate a variety of birds and animals in various stages of recovery. The hospital and nursery with its small enclosures and humidicribs accommodates animals like kangaroos, joeys, wallabies, possums, reptiles and birds. In the larger outdoor enclosures there are wombats, kangaroos, koalas (there is also a special koala breeding programme), wallabies, deer, echidnas and dingoes. A host of aviaries house a variety of native bird life. And a special area has also been established to house penguins and seals.

Over a period of 25 years, thousands of creatures have been rehabilitated and released back into the bush and the sea. The Sanctuary receives no government funding assistance relying solely on entry fees and donations from the public, along with income derived from extensive pet boarding facilities.

Open: 10 am to 5 pm, daily

Where: Taits Rd

Tel: 5254 2484

OCEAN GROVE

Ocean Grove is the largest town on the Bellarine Peninsula, and it has grown rapidly over the last twenty years. Many residents commute to Geelong, but it is still a thriving holiday resort, blessed with one of the longest, safest sandy beaches in the state, as well as the Barwon estuary. It is believed the first European settler was William Bonsey in 1854, but Ocean Grove's development is really thanks to a group of American Methodists with a dream....

In the 1870s the American Methodist church established a successful beach camp known as Ocean Grove in New Jersey, USA. In 1879 the Methodists took their idea abroad; a temporary camp at Point Lonsdale attracted decent crowds so in 1882 it was decided to acquire land nearby for an Australian Ocean Grove. The Methodists ensured there were permanent covenants prohibiting the sale of alcohol, and over 30 streets were laid out and named after famous Methodists. The ambitious plans were not fully realized however, and the town ended up developing as a normal holiday centre – with the important exception that there is still no hotel! The Methodist Church that was built in 1888 at 100 Eggleston St is now the Ocean Grove Uniting Church.

Ocean Grove has a wide variety of cool weather tourist activities. See the Parks & Reserves chapter for information on the important **Ocean Grove Nature Reserve**, one of the last remaining untouched woodland environments on the Peninsula, and the internationally-significant **Lake Connewarre State Game Reserve**.

A MAZE 'N' THINGS

This is one of Australia's largest wooden mazes and you can spend as long as it takes to find your way out before enjoying a puzzle and jigsaw centre, a croquet court and a putting green. There is a kiosk, a playground and barbecues

Open: 11 am to 5 pm, Mon to Fri; 10 am to 6 pm, Sat and Sun;

Where: cnr Grubb Rd and Bellarine Hwy, Wallington

Tel: 5250 2669.

ADVENTURE PARK

Adventure Park is one of Victoria's premier amusement parks with over 19 adventure activities. These include a 115-metre raft waterslide, go-karts, jumping castles (including one for adults), volleyball, a merry-go-round, paddleboats, flying foxes, an archery range, Adventure Island mini-golf, aqua bikes, canoes, the Paddle Pop Express Train and the Adventure Playground – all set in extensive parkland. There's a kiosk and café, plus barbecues.

Open: 10 am to 5 pm, daily except Tue

Cost: there are special winter admission prices; summer admission is $19.50 for adults, and $15 for children under 1.2 metres

Where: 1251 Bellarine Hwy

Tel: 5250 2756

www.adventurepark.com.au.

Top: Joe Mortelliti, Raffs Beach
Bottom: George Stawicki, Barwon Heads and Ocean Grove

Left: George Stawicki, Point Lonsdale
Right: George Stawicki, Point Lonsdale
Opposite: George Stawicki, Point Lonsdale

POINT LONSDALE

Point Lonsdale is a quiet little town with a dramatic location at the western end of the Bellarine Peninsula. It overlooks the entrance to Port Phillip Bay where the sheltered waters of the bay meet the surging swells of Bass Strait. This 3.5 km stretch of water is known as the Rip and it is recognized as one of the most dangerous stretches of water on the Australian coastline.

The Rip has claimed numerous wrecks and the European history of Point Lonsdale begins with attempts to make the passage safer. A signal station was established in 1852, and after the famous clipper Lightning struck a reef in 1862 an old wooden lighthouse from Queenscliff was re-erected at Point Lonsdale. A new concrete lighthouse, believed to be the first reinforced concrete building in Victoria, was built in 1902.

Below the lighthouse is another Pt Lonsdale icon, the pier, which was built in 1890 to house a lifeboat. The end of the pier, which housed the lifeboat, was swept away in storms in 1984, but it's still a favourite with fishermen. There are also a number of gun and searchlight emplacements that were constructed for the defence of Port Phillip during WWII.

The township itself remained undeveloped until shortly before the extension of the railway line from Geelong to Queenscliff in 1879. In 1876 there were land sales at Point Lonsdale, and in 1885 a boarding house was opened.

Between WWI and WWII there were six or seven guesthouses and all but two have gone. One that survives is the newly refurbished **Point Lonsdale Guesthouse** (previously known as the Terminus Guesthouse) dating from 1895. Once considerably smaller than Queenscliff, Point Lonsdale is now bigger, and new development means it is continuing to push into the wetland area to the west.

Point Lonsdale is now a favourite with well-to-do retirees from the Western District and Melbourne, and it is a prosperous little town. There are a number of cafes in Point Lonsdale Rd, the main street, where it's now possible to find good coffee and quality light meals. The small shopping centre overlooks the sheltered **Front Beach**, inside the heads, which is a favourite with families and snorkelers. There are great rock pools. There's easy snorkeling inshore, but there's also world class diving in the Rip, where the colour and diversity rivals that on the Great Barrier Reef. For more information, see **Point Lonsdale** under the **Port Phillip Marine National Park** section in the **Parks & Reserves** chapter.

The ocean **Back Beach** is a hot walk over large sand dunes and it can be quite exposed. It can also have excellent, sometimes dangerous, surf; the beach is patrolled in summer. The **Rip View Lookout** near the lighthouse is an unmatched viewpoint for the daily drama of the Rip.

Top: George Stawicki, Queenscliff
Bottom: George Stawicki, Queenscliff
Opposite: Historical Queesncliff print,
courtesy Queenscliffe Historical Museum

QUEENSCLIFF

The heritage township of Queenscliff gives the impression of being an island time capsule. Viewed from the ridge behind Swan Bay, Shortland Bluff is almost completely surrounded by water, and with its profile defined by lighthouses, Norfolk Pines, and Victorian architecture it seems as if much of the 20th century has passed it by.

Queenscliff is only connected to Point Lonsdale by a slender sand dune isthmus called The Narrows, which separates Port Phillip Bay from Swan Bay. Its economy has depended on three mainstays: the government, fishing and tourism. But after the demise of the bay steamers in the 1930s Queenscliff dropped out of tourist fashion. The government departments and fishermen stayed on, but tourism became a very low key business, based around sailing and fishing. The day tripper's numbers dropped to a trickle and the grand hotels were largely empty for sixty years.

Queenscliff has always been a Government town. It has provided postal, customs, health and telegraph services, lighthouse and signal services, military and defence establishments and the – ongoing - sea pilot service. European settlement of Queenscliff began only one year after Port Phillip was surveyed because it was immediately clear that the Rip was a major hazard. In 1838 a pilot service was established: four men in a whaleboat ventured out in all weathers.

In 1842 the first lighthouse was built out of sandstone quarried from Shortland Bluff, and the same year the first boat excursions from Melbourne were recorded. In 1852 the Geelong Town Council petitioned Governor La Trobe to establish a Post Office, Customs Office and jetty; later that same year they also suggested a town be established as a place of recreation for the citizens of Geelong. La Trobe agreed and named the town Queenscliff in honour of Queen Victoria, and later actually built himself a holiday house in the town.

The fishing industry took off in the 1860s and a sizeable fishing fleet developed. Some of the fishermen were Chinese anglers who supplied dried fish to their countrymen on the goldfields, but many other nationalities, including Maoris, Italians, Dutchmen, and Frenchmen, were involved in the industry. They built their huts on the sand flats around the current location of the railway station.

In 1863 the famous black lighthouse was built. Fort Queenscliff was primarily built between 1879 and 1889, after the Crimean War, when the wealthy citizens of Melbourne feared a Russian (yes Russian!) invasion. By 1886, Port Phillip was the most heavily fortified port in the southern hemisphere, with Fort Queenscliff the command centre for a string of forts and gun batteries around the bay. The fort, including many historic buildings, is open for public tours and the fort museum has one of Australia's largest collections of war memorabilia and WWI and WWII guns.

Top: George Stawicki, Queenscliff
Bottom: George Stawicki, Queenscliff
Opposite: Robert Bole, Queenscliff

Although it has never fired a shot in anger, Fort Queenscliff may have come under attack... According to the Queenscliffe Historical Museum, on 1 September 1942, at 2.15 am a certain Gunner Hulston was found missing from his sentry post. Heavy marks were discovered on the beach and a servicemen searching for Hulston was fired upon and wounded. Nine days later Hulston's body was found in the sea. The mystery remains unsolved, but one theory proposes Hulston was captured and killed by raiders from a Japanese submarine.

Partly to support the military presence a railway line was built from Geelong to Queenscliff in 1879. This still operates to/from Drysdale on weekends. Thanks to the train services and the bay steamers tourism boomed through the 1880s; Geelong visitors would make the journey by train in an hour, and the steamers from Melbourne only took two hours. The boom led to the construction of grand hotels: in 1881, the Baillieu Hotel, later renamed the Ozone, was built; in 1883 the Vue Grand was built (it was refashioned in 1927 after a fire); and in 1887 the Queenscliff Hotel in Gellibrand St was built.

Today Queenscliff is once more a fashionable tourist destination, and the gourmet capital of the Bellarine Peninsula. The grand hotels have been revived and have become luxury weekend escapes once again. Hesse St is lined with cafes, expensive shops and galleries. The environment also remains a key drawcard; see separate sections on the **Port Phillip Marine National Park** and **Swan Bay**; the **Queenscliff Golf Club**; and **Diving & Snorkeling.**

Once again, sea transport has played a role in creating Queenscliff's prosperity. While not as instantly appealing as paddle steamers, modern car ferries now ply hourly between Queenscliff and Sorrento, linking the Mornington and Bellarine peninsulas and creating a number of intriguing options for travelers.

BELLARINE PENINSULA RAILWAY

The Queenscliff Railway Station in Symonds St, is now home to the Bellarine Peninsula Railway which is run by the Geelong Steam Preservation Society. It has a collection of vintage steam locomotives and carriages which take passengers on scenic trips to Drysdale and Laker's Siding, taking in views of Swan Bay, the Bellarine Hills, Corio Bay and Port Phillip Bay. Return trips to Drysdale take 1.75 hours, to Laker' Siding and return takes 40 minutes.

Open: Sun, and Tue and Thur in school holidays

Cost: Single/return to Laker's Siding is $5/10 for adults; $2.50/5 for children; single/return to Drysdale is $8/16 for adults; $4/8 for children

Tel: 5258 2069

www.bpr.org.au

DIVING, SNORKELING & SEAL SWIMS

The snorkeling and diving around Queenscliff is amongst the best in the world. To cap it all it is possible to snorkel with friendly Australian fur seals and dolphins. The **Visitor Information Centre** can provide further information. Also see the **Diving & Snorkeling** chapter.

Top: George Stawicki, Queenscliff
Bottom: George Stawicki, Point Lonsdale and Queenscliff

FISHING & FISHING CHARTERS

Queenscliff is a noted surf, boat and pier fishing area. Popular fishing areas are Queenscliff pier, the rock walls and jetties of Queenscliff anchorage and the sheltered waters of Swan Bay. The Visitor Information Centre can provide information on a number of fishing charter operators run trips to reefs around Port Phillip, into the Rip or beyond into Bass Strait.

MARINE DISCOVERY CENTRE

The Marine Discovery Centre is an educational facility that features the wonders of southern Australia's marine environment. The centre offers an insight into local marine life, has aquariums and touch tanks, and organises boat trips, snorkeling and rockpool rambles. The centre conducts special programs for adults and children throughout the year during school holidays and on weekends.

Open: 10 am to 4 pm, school holidays

Tel: 5258 3344

QUEENSCLIFFE HISTORICAL MUSEUM

The Queenscliffe Historical Museum is next door to the old post office. Run by enthusiastic and knowledgeable volunteers, the museum has an outstanding collection illustrating the history of the region. They also have a number of brochures describing walking tours around the town. The collection is well organized and displayed, and can be categorized into four main elements: photographs, recorded history, lace and textiles, and artifacts. There are approximately 8000 photographic prints dating from 1862, and covering shipwrecks, bay steamers, the fishing industry, and family albums. Black and white copies of the photos can be ordered at a small cost. The historical records include diaries, family records and early newspapers, a Cobb & Co timetable, and so on. The museum also has an extensive collection of artifacts from daily life in the homes, hotels and guesthouses.

Open: 2 pm to 4 pm, weekends and most weekdays

Cost: donation

Where: next door to Post Office, Hesse St

Tel: 5258 2511

FORT QUEENSCLIFF

Fort Queenscliff was designed to attack enemy shipping, and to withstand a small-scale land attack, so it has a surprisingly medieval appearance. There is a dry moat, once crossed by drawbridge, a fort wall complete with rifle loopholes, and a castellated keep. Today there is a subterranean museum of military memorabilia and tours are available on weekends.

Open: tours at 1 pm and 3 pm, weekends and public holidays, daily in school holidays

Where: King St

Tel: 5258 1488

OCEAN VIEW, SHORTLANDS BLUFF

Continue past the fort at the end of Hesse St, for a viewpoint behind the fort that gives a commanding view of the Rip.

OZONE HOTEL.

The commanding Ozone Hotel is a Queenscliff icon, and has been a favourite with both holiday-makers and locals since 1881. Victorian grandeur is captured throughout the hotel, and the magnificent Grand Dining Room serves exceptionally fine food and wine. Many guest rooms have ocean views, all feature Victorian-style décor and ensuite facilities. In summer there's live jazz in the courtyard garden every Sunday afternoon.

42 Gellibrand Street Queenscliff 3225

Tel: [03] 5258 1011 **Fax:** [03] 5258 3712

Email: info@ozonehotel.com.au **www.ozonehotel.com.au**

Top: George Stawicki, Indented Head
Bottom: George Stawicki, St Leonards
Opposite left: George Stawicki, Indented Head
Opposite right: George Stawicki, Indented Head

ST LEONARDS & INDENTED HEAD

Originally, the entire Bellarine Peninsula was known as Indented Head, named by Mathew Flinders when he viewed it from Arthur's Seat on the other side of the bay, perhaps in a reference to the dent in the peninsula made by Swan Lake. Flinders was the first European to camp on the foreshore, before his excursion to the You Yangs. Then came John Batman, the founder of Melbourne, who made his camp at St Leonards in 1835, before moving on to his meeting with destiny at the northern end of the bay. The escaped convict William Buckley marched in to Batman's St Leonards camp after spending 32 years with the Wathaurang (see the separate **William Buckley** section).

James Langdon took up his St. Leonards pastoral station in the area in 1849, possibly taking the name from the town of that name in Sussex, England. Holiday makers started camping on the foreshore in substantial numbers at least as early as 1920.

Today the foreshores of both St Leonards and Indented Head remain popular camping destinations; the sheltered beaches are ideal for families and people who like messing about in boats. There are a number of boat ramps, and sailing, waterskiing, fishing and snorkelling (especially around the wreck of the Ozone) are all popular.

St Leonards backs on to the Swan Bay wetlands and the **Edward Point State Faunal Reserve** (see separate section in the **Parks & Reserves** chapter). There are several locations that were used in the ABC's popular Sea Change series, including the St Leonards Hotel.

On a clear day, the curve of the planet means the skyscrapers of Melbourne seem to rise disconcertingly from the waters of the bay, from just below the edge of the horizon.

Top: George Stawicki, Portarlington
Bottom: George Stawicki, Portarlington
Opposite left: George Stawicki, Portarlington
Opposite right: Portarlington Mill, courtesy National Trust

PORTARLINGTON

Portarlington was once just over an hour from Williamstown by steamer (see the **Steamer** section). With sheltered north facing beaches, sea baths, gardens and great views over the bay to the You Yangs, Mt Macedon and the Dandenongs, it was an immensely popular destination for day trippers. The Grand Hotel was built in 1888 to cater to thirsty Melbournians.

Improved roads and a fresh appreciation for smaller communities have seen Portarlington flourish in recent years, although except for a couple of summer weekends it is still much quieter than it was in its glory days. There are several excellent places to eat, and a number of nearby wineries.

The pier – built to serve the flour mill and the local farmers – led to the first tourist boom and it is still central to the life of the town. The original Portarlington fishing fleet was crewed largely by Chinese; today there are still a number of boats, and a growing aquaculture industry based on mussel farming. Fresh mussels are sold straight out of the water, off the boat at the pier.

Portarlington Mill

The National Trust owned Portarlington Mill is one of Victoria's once ubiquitous flour mills. The four-storey building was built from locally-quarried sandstone in 1857 on what is thought to be a former corroboree site. A small jetty was built on the nearby beach and boats carried the flour and bran to larger vessels in deeper waters. The closure of the mill in 1874 reflected the successful establishment of wheat-growing in western Victoria – the Portarlington Mill and number of other iconic flour mills in central Victoria were made redundant at about the same time. The enterprising builder of the mill, Tom Widdicombe bought the redundant mill and converted it into a brickworks and the building has had many other roles over the years. Now fully restored it contains displays relating to the history of the mill and the area.

Where: Turner Court off Sproat St

Open: noon to 4 pm, Sat, Sun and public holidays

Tel: 5259 2804

Top: George Stawicki, approaching Clifton Springs
Bottom: George Stawicki, Drysdale and Clifton Springs
Opposite: Joe Mortelliti, Clifton Springs

DRYSDALE & CLIFTON SPRINGS

Drysdale and Clifton Springs have a rich history, beginning with the Wathaurang people, who, as late as 1855, were known to have camped around the large permanent water holes that lie near the centre of town. In fact the first European name for the district was the Water Holes. As these lakes were the only fresh water between Geelong and Portarlington, they became an important stopover point on the three hour (!) journey between the two towns, and a natural focal point for the peninsula.

Two of the early pioneers were women: Anne Drysdale, after whom the town is now named, and Caroline Newcomb, after whom a Geelong suburb is named. Anne Drysdale was born in Scotland. She arrived at Port Phillip in 1840, well educated, deeply religious, unmarried, 47 years old, and determined to be a successful squatter. The much younger Carolyn Newcomb arrived in Melbourne in 1836 when only two houses existed, as the governess to John Batman's family. She too was religious and well educated, but also an accomplished rider, high-spirited and strong-willed. In 1837, when she was 25, she moved from Melbourne to work for the Thomson family who had settled at today's Belmont. Here she met Anne Drysdale.

This meeting led to an extraordinary partnership and friendship that lasted until the death of Anne at the age of 61 in 1853. These intrepid pioneers carved a successful farm out of a frontier where there were no roads, no houses, and few Europeans, let alone educated European ladies. In 1849 they built themselves a fine home in the Gothic Revival style – Coriyule – which overlooks the bay just to the west of Clifton Springs. After Anne's death Caroline married a Rev. James Dodgson in 1861 and continued to live at Coriyule until her own death in 1874.

Drysdale became the administrative and commercial centre of the Shire of Bellarine (which was formed in 1865) until it was combined with Geelong in 1993. The township is now contiguous with Clifton Springs.

Mineral springs with iron, magnesia and sulphur were discovered to the west of Drysdale in 1870 on a property called Clifton, and the springs area was named Fairy Dell. To take full advantage of the springs, in 1880 a 20-room hotel, salt water baths and a pier (for the bay steamers) was constructed. The hotel was burnt down in 1923 but rebuilt three years later. In 1957 it was acquired by developers and transformed into a country club with a high quality golf course that was the hub of a new residential development.

Drysdale has a number of fine old buildings, including the 1880 Court House, now home to Bellarine Historical Society and an interesting museum which is open every Sunday from January to April from 1.30 pm to 4.30 pm, and the 1st Sunday of every month from May to December. Drysdale is the western terminal for the **Bellarine Peninsula Railway** (see the **Queenscliff** section for details), and a number of fine wineries including **Kilgour Estate** and **Scotchmans Hill** (see the **Wine** section for details) are nearby.

BUSINESS LISTINGS

ANAKIE			
Del Rios of Mt Anakie	Wineries	2320 Ballan Rd	03 9497 4644
Mt Anakie Winery SEE AD ON PAGE 111 & 189	Wineries	130 Staughton Vale Rd	03 5284 1256
Straughton Vale Winery SEE AD ON PAGE 107 & 190	Wineries	Cnr Ballan & Staughton Vale Rd	03 5284 1477
BALLIANG			
Ripley Park	Accommodation	Gilmores Road	03 5369 4222
BANNOCKBURN			
Railway Hotel	Dining	High St	03 5281 1230
Bannockburn Newsagency	Retail	Shop 12/ 6 High St	03 5281 1625
BARWON HEADS			
1 River Pde	Accommodation	1 River Pde	0416 032 929
Agapanthus Cottage	Accommodation	6 Ozone Road	0412 102 145
Barwon Heads Caravan Park	Accommodation	Ewing Blyth Drive	03 5254 1115
Barwon Heads Hotel	Accommodation	Bridge Road	03 5254 2201
Barwon Shores	Accommodation	2/67 Hitchcock Ave	04 0946 7322
Golightly Beach House	Accommodation	37 Hitchcock Ave	0418 135 769
"Hawley, Barwon Heads"	Accommodation	9 Thorn Street	03 9329 5233
Kaneira Beach House	Accommodation	42 Hitchcock Ave	03 9690 4719
Lill Brey on Barwon	Accommodation	2A Ozone Road	03 5243 8808
Marg Austin Getaway Rentals	Accommodation	19 Hitchcock Ave	03 5254 2416
Monomeeth	Accommodation	33 Flinders Pde	03 9572 2334
Moonah Beach House	Accommodation	9 Reid St	03 5254 3145
Rondor Caravan Park	Accommodation	Sheepwash Road	03 5254 2753
Seahaven Village	Accommodation	1-7 Geelong Road	03 5254 1066
Tobermory Cottage	Accommodation	16 Bridge Rd	03 5254 3145
Friends of the Lobster Pot Inc	Attractions	Jetty Road	03 5254 1115
At the Heads	Dining	Jetty Rd	03 5254 1277
Peppercorn Foods	Dining	47 Hitchcock Ave	03 5254 2602
Barwon Heads Hotel	Dining	Bridge Road	03 5254 2201
Thirteenth Beach Golf Links Ltd	Dining	Barwon Heads Road	03 5254 2922
Jirrahlinga - Koala & Wildlife Sanctuary	Eco Tourism	Taits Road	03 5254 2484
Barwon Heads Golf Club	Golf Courses	Golf Links Road	03 5254 2302

Thirteenth Beach Golf Links Ltd	Golf Courses	Barwon Heads Road	03 5254 2922
Barwon Heads Newsagency	Retail	43 Hitchcock Ave	03 5254 2260
Beach Books Barwon Heads	Retail	46 Hitchcock Ave	03 5254 2739
Klaassen Charters	Tours and Transport	9 Dudley Crt	03 5254 2410
BATESFORD			
El Dorado Tourist Park	Accommodation	360 Ballarat Road	03 5276 1386
Lilydale House Home Hosting	Accommodation	100 Dog Rocks Road	03 5276 1302
Moorabool Estate	Wineries	45 Dog Rocks Rd	03 5276 1536
BELLARINE			
The Green Anchor	Accommodation	295 Scotchman's Rd	03 5259 3995
Views' End	Accommodation	265 Scotchman's Rd	03 5253 1695
Bellarine Estate	Wineries	2270 Portarlington Rd	03 5259 3310
Kilgour Estate Winery	Wineries	85 McAdams Lane	03 5251 2223
Spray Farm	Wineries	2275 Portarlington Rd	03 5251 3176
BELLBRAE			
Bellbrae Harvest SEE AD ON PAGE 189	Dining	45 Portreath Road	03 52662100
Bellbrae Estate, Longboard SEE AD ON PAGE 189	Winery	520 Great Ocean Road	03 5264 8480
BREAMLEA			
Breamlea Caravan Park	Accommodation	Horwood Drive	03 5264 1352
CERES			
R L Aviation	Tourism Services	195 Merrawarp Rd	03 5249 1387
CLIFTON SPRINGS			
Bay and Mountain View	Accommodation	129 Bayshore Ave	03 5251 1463
Bayshore Holiday Rental	Accommodation	142 Bayshore Ave	03 9822 8877
Clifton Springs Golf Club	Golf Courses	Springs Road	03 5251 3391
CONNEWARRE			
Breamlea Country Style Accommodation	Accommodation	80 Bluestone School Rd	03 5264 1774
Skydive City	Sports Club	Barwon Heads Airport - 1405 Barwon Heads Rd	03 5254 1467
South Barwon Air Services	Tours and Transport	Barwon Heads Airport-1405 Barwon Heads Rd	03 5254 2338
The Minya	Wineries	"Glengower CottageDans Road"	03 5264 1397
CURLEWIS			
Curlewis Golf Club	Golf Courses	Portarlington Road	03 5251 2534
Curlewis Winery	Wineries	55 Navarre Rd	03 5250 4567
Bellarine Bayview Bed & Breakfast	Accommodation	"Lot 7, Wisbey Court"	03 5251 1983
DRYSDALE			

■	Bellarine Bellevue House	Accommodation	77 Princess St	0418 556 841
■	Eagleview B&B	Accommodation	32-50 Belchers Rd	03 5251 2397
■	Tuckerberry Hill	Attractions	35 Becks Road	03 5251 3468
■	Zanoni's Café Wine Bar	Dining	16a High St	03 5253 3086
■	Drysdale Newsagency & Tattslotto	Retail	14 High St	03 5251 2776
■	Hommy's Quality Meats	Retail	16 High St	03 5251 2270
■	Leura Park Estate Vineyard	Wineries	1400 Portarlington Rd	03 5253 3180
■	Scotchmans Hill Vineyards	Wineries	190 Scotchman's Road	03 5251 3176
ELCHO HEIGHTS				
■	Tower Hill	Accommodation	45 Oswald Ave	0408 221 600
FYANSFORD				
■	Truffleduck at Balmoral Receptions	Conference Centre	66 Hyland Street	03 5229 7503
GEELONG				
■	Aaron Lee Waterfront Apartments	Accommodation	30 Western Beach Rd	03 5222 7733
■	Abbotswood Motor Inn	Accommodation	308-310 High Street	03 5243 0122
■	Aberdeen Motor Inn & Restaurant	Accommodation	9 Aberdeen Street	03 5221 2177
■	Admiralty Motor Inn	Accommodation	66 McKillop Street	03 5221 4288
■	Alexandra Apartments	Accommodation	17 Alexandra Ave	0419 320 955
■	Ardara House	Accommodation	4 Aberdeen St	03 5229 6024
■	Aristocrat Waurnvale Motel	Accommodation	90 Princes Highway	03 5241 8211
■	Austin Park Townhouse	Accommodation	15 England St	0409 931 396
■	Ayrbank Bed & Breakfast	Accommodation	170 Bellarine St	03 5229 7922
■	Barwon Caravan Park	Accommodation	153-163 Barrabool Road	03 5243 3842
■	Barwon Valley Lodge	Accommodation	99-109 Barrabool Road	03 5244 2111
■	Bay City Motel	Accommodation	231 Malop Street	03 5221 1933
■	Baywoodbyne B & B	Accommodation	41 The Esplanade	03 5278 2658
■	Carlton Central Accommodation	Accommodation	21 Malop St	03 5229 1955
■	City Southside Caravan Park	Accommodation	87 Barrabool Road	03 5243 3788
■	Colonial Lodge Motel	Accommodation	57 Fyans Street	03 5223 2266
■	Comfort Inn Eastern Sands Motel	Accommodation	1 Bellerine Street	03 5221 5577
■	Comfort Inn Parkside	Accommodation	68 High Street	03 5243 6766
■	Corio Bay Motel	Accommodation	292-296 Princess Highway	03 5275 1489
■	Ebony Quill Spa Cottages	Accommodation	620 Princes Hwy	03 5266 1394
■	"Four Points By Sheraton, Geelong"	Accommodation	10-14 Eastern Beach Rd	03 5223 1377
■	Garden Cottage	Accommodation	1/11 Meakin Street	03 5975 7529

■	Gatehouse on Ryrie	Accommodation	83 Yarra St	0417 545 196
■	Gateway Hotel	Accommodation	218 Princes Hwy	03 5275 1091
■	Geelong Apartments	Accommodation	90 McKillop St	03 5221 5959
■	Geelong Caravan Park	Accommodation	Princes Highway	03 5243 7298
■	Geelong Motor Inn	Accommodation	Cnr Princes Hwy & Kooyong Rd	03 5222 4777
■	Geelong Riverview Tourist Park	Accommodation	59 Barrabool Rd	03 5243 6225
■	Golden Palms Motel	Accommodation	234 Torquay Road	03 5243 1077
■	Grove Manor Apartments	Accommodation	9 Rubens Crt (Do not use for postage)	03 5241 4447
■	Hacienda Motel	Accommodation	15 Mt Pleasant Road	03 5243 5844
■	Hyatt Apartments	Accommodation	63 Fyans Street	03 5274 9192
■	Irish Murphys	Accommodation	30 Aberdeen St	03 5221 4335
■	Jokers on Ryrie	Accommodation	211 Ryrie St	03 5229 1104
■	Kardinia Geelong Apartments	Accommodation	10 Swanston St	0407 443 770
■	Kardinia Park Motel	Accommodation	422 Latrobe Tce	03 5221 5188
■	Kennett River Beach House	Accommodation	6 Ryrie Street	03 5229 8233
■	Kiloran Motel	Accommodation	158-172 Colac Rd	03 5243 6333
■	Lintyn on Shannon	Accommodation	91 Shannon Ave	0407 233 709
■	"Mercure Hotel, Geelong"	Accommodation	Cnr Gheringhap & Myers Sts	03 5223 6200
■	National Hotel	Accommodation	191 Moorabool St	0410 529 935
■	Nireeda Apartments on Clare	Accommodation	1-3 Clare St	03 5221 0566
■	Oberon Apartments	Accommodation	9 Pevensey Cres	0419 29 8445
■	Parkwood Motel	Accommodation	Cnr Shannon Ave and Ballarat Rd	03 5278 5477
■	Pevensey House 1892	Accommodation	17 Pevensey Cres	03 5224 2810
■	Rippleside Park Motor Inn	Accommodation	67 Melbourne Rd	03 5278 2017
■	Riverglen Caravan Park	Accommodation	75 Barrabool Road	03 5243 5505
■	Rose Garden Motel	Accommodation	14 - 16 Settlement Road	03 5241 9441
■	Sea Mist Holiday Apartments	Accommodation	62-64 Western Beach Rd	03 5222 2447
■	Shannon Motor Inn	Accommodation	283-285 Shannon Ave	03 5222 4355
■	Sphinx Entertainment Centre	Accommodation	2 Thompson Rd	03 5278 2911
■	Sundowner Motor Inn Geelong	Accommodation	13 The Esplanade	03 5244 7700
■	Sydney Ave Cottage	Accommodation	18 Sydney Ave	03 5221 8260
■	T & S Accommodation	Accommodation	59 Elizabeth St	0402 568 927
■	The Haymarket	Accommodation	244 Moorabool Steet	03 5221 1174
■	The Peninsula	Accommodation	195 Queenscliff Rd	03 5248 2606
■	The Waterfront Apartments	Accommodation	"2302 / 2 Yarra St, Eastern Beach"	0409 931 396

Verner Place	Accommodation	171 Verner Street	03 5229 9970
Waterfront 2507	Accommodation	"Unit 2507, 2 Yarra St"	0417 379 117
Armor Antiques	Antiques	42 Corio St	03 5221 4296
Evergreen Antiques Gifts & Garden Centre	Antiques	313 Pakington St	03 5221 7472
Hermitage Antiques	Antiques	"The Wintergarden, 51 McKillop St"	03 5222 3193
Kennys Antiques	Antiques	71-75 Vines Rd	03 5278 6110
Moorabool Antique Galleries	Antiques	16-18 Ryrie St	03 5229 2970
Pegasus Antiques	Antiques	550 Latrobe Tce	03 5221 8290
The Mill	Antiques	3 Mackay Street	03 5278 9989
Geelong Heritage Centre	Association	51 Lt Malop Street	03 5227 0970
Barwon Grange - National Trust	Attractions	Fernleigh Street	03 5221 3906
Baywalk Bollards	Attractions	Eastern Beach	03 5222 6110
Eastern Beach	Attractions	Eastern Beach	03 5227 0342
Eastern Beach Train Hire	Attractions	"Waterfront, Geelong"	03 5243 4306
Geelong Maritime Museum	Attractions	"The Stables, Osborne House, Swinburne Street"	03 5277 3808
Narana Creations	Attractions	410 Torquay Road	03 5241 5700
National Wool Museum	Attractions	26 Moorabool Street	03 5227 0701
Old Geelong Gaol	Attractions	Cnr Myers & Swanston Sts	03 5221 8292
The Arena	Attractions		03 5278 3092
The Carousel	Attractions	Eastern Beach	03 5224 1547
The Heights (National Trust)	Attractions	140 Aphrasia St	03 5221 3510
Waterfront Geelong	Attractions	Eastern Beach	03 5227 0342
Bay City Cabs/Murrell Chauffeur Drive	Car Hire	11-15 Douro Street	13 2227
Endeavour Coach Company Pty Ltd	Car Hire	14A Mundy Street	03 5223 2517
Galaxy Limousines	Car Hire	176 Minerva Rd	03 5222 4535
Geelong Radio Cabs Co-operative	Car Hire	21-25 Church Street	03 5278 4776
McHarry's Buslines Pty Ltd	Car Hire	6 Reeves Court	03 5223 2111
Rent A Tinny	Car Hire	3 Breakwater Road	03 5222 3222
Avis Rent a Car	Car Rental	344 Latrobe Tce	03 5332 8310
Budget Rent a Car	Car Rental	137 Mercer Street	03 5222 4588
Europcar - Geelong	Car Rental	48 Mercer Sreet	03 5229 8188
Hertz Car Rental	Car Rental	323 Latrobe Terrace	03 5222 4433
Rent - a - Bomb	Car Rental	12 Mercer Street	03 5229 9122
Deakin Management Centre	Conference Centre	Deakin University	03 5227 3000
Mecure Hotel	Conference Centre	Cnr Myers & Gheringhap St	03 5221 6844

Empire Grill	Conference Centre	66 McKillop Street	03 5223 2132
Geelong Performing Arts Centre	Conference Centre	50 Little Malop St	03 5225 1200
Savvas	Conference Centre	51 Moorabool St	03 5229 3703
Sladen House	Conference Centre	410 Packington St	03 5222 1214
Sundowner Motor Inn Geelong	Conference Centre	13 The Esplanade	1800 654 576
The Geelong Wintergarden Café	Conference Centre	51 McKillop St	03 5221 3744
Geelong Conference Centre	Conference Centre	"Adams Court, Eastern Park"	03 5226 2121
Kardinia Heights Centre	Conference Centre	Cnr Anakie Rd & Ballarat Hwy	03 5272 2003
The Beach House	Conference Centre	Eastern Beach	03 5221 8322
2 Faces Restaurant SEE AD ON PAGE 189	Dining	8 Malop Street	03 5229 4546
Bamboleo	Dining	86 Little Malop Street	03 5229 2458
Barwon Club	Dining	509 Moorabool St	03 5221 4584
Bazils Café-Restaurant	Dining	2/100 Western Beach Rd	03 5229 8965
Bazils Too	Dining	"Shop 9, 65 Barrabool Rd"	03 52419311
Black Sheep Café	Dining	Cnr Moorabool & Brougham Sts	03 5223 2536
Café Botticelli	Dining	111 Pakington St	03 5229 8292
Café Brulee	Dining	197 Pakington St	03 5229 1858
Cats	Dining	90 Little Malop St	03 5229 3077
Empire Grill SEE AD ON PAGE 189	Dining	66 McKillop Street	03 5223 2132
Fishermen's Pier Restaurant	Dining	Yarra Street	03 5222 4100
The Geelong Wintergarden Café	Dining	51 McKillop St	03 5221 3744
Gilligan's Fish & Chips	Dining	100 Western Beach	03 5222 3200
Giuseppe's Café	Dining	149 Pakington St	03 5223 2187
Hi Sushi	Dining	76 Malop St	03 5223 3288
Home House	Dining	40-43 Moorabool St	03 5222 7333
Le Parisien	Dining	15 Eastern Beach Rd	03 5229 3110
Lipari Espresso Bar	Dining	10 Union Street	03 5222 5600
Pancake Kitchen	Dining	48 Moorabool Street	03 5229 7888
The Pink Fish	Dining	88 Little Malop Street	03 5229 8845
Sailors' Rest	Dining	3 Moorabool Street	03 5224 2241
Spinnakers	Dining	1 Bellerine Street	03 5222 4113
sticks & grace	Dining	4/337 Pakington St	03 5224 2900
St Georges Workers Club	Dining	212 Pakington St	03 5221 3162
Sun Bo Chinese Restaurant	Dining	39 Gheringhap Street	03 5222 3580
Tarts on Pakington	Dining	140 Pakington Street	03 5222 2889

The Barking Dog Wine Bar Café	Dining	126 Pakington St	03 5229 2889
The Beach House	Dining	Eastern Beach Reserve	03 5221 8322
Tonic Lounge Bar & Restaurant	Dining	5 James Street	03 5229 8899
Ushers	Dining	93 Yarra St	03 5229 7529
Warung Bali	Dining	146a Shannon Ave	03 5229 1252
Winters	Dining	330 Pakington Street	03 5221 8832
Wharf Shed Café	Dining	15 Eastern Beach Rd	03 5221 6645
The Ying & I	Dining	136 Malop St	03 5222 1737
Zest SEE AD ON PAGE 117 & 188	Dining	188 Moorabool St	03 5229 1388
The Geelong College SEE AD ON PAGE 43	Education	Aberdeen Street & Talbot Street	03 5226 3111
Buckley's The Entertainment Centre	Entertainment Centre	54 Fellmongers Rd	03 5248 4866
Club Cats - Geelong Football Club SEE AD ON PAGE 188	Entertainment Centre	Kardinia Park	03 5225 2355
Geelong Bowling Lanes	Entertainment Centre	49 Reynolds Rd	03 5241 2200
Geelong Performing Arts Centre	Entertainment Centre	50 Lt Malop Street	03 5225 1213
Norlane Hotel	Entertainment Centre	2-8 Princes Highway	03 5278 2423
The Sphinx SEE AD ON PAGE 190	Entertainment Centre	2 Thompson Rd	03 5278 2911
Village Cinemas Geelong	Entertainment Centre	194 Ryrie Street	03 5229 3006
Aerospace Foundation of Australia Ltd	Event Group	BLDG 53 Avalon Airport	03 5282 4400
Geelong Agricultural & Pastoral Society Inc	Event Group	79 Breakwater Rd	03 5221 1707
Geelong Speed Trials Inc	Event Group	5 Upper Skene Street	03 9593 7735
Pako Festa 'Celebrating Cultural Diversity'	Event Group	153 Pakington Street	03 5221 6044
The Geelong Eisteddfod Society Inc	Event Group	PO Box 719	03 5243 3970
Brim Brim Gallery	Galleries	560a Latrobe Tce	03 5221 8874
Gordon Gallery	Galleries	2 Fenwick St	03 5229 3645
Murston House	Galleries	82 Ryrie St	03 5229 9811
Narana Creations SEE AD ON PAGE 81 & 189	Galleries	410 Torquay Rd	03 5241 5700
Ryrie St Art Gallery	Galleries	Ryrie St	03 5229 7805
Shearers Arms Gallery	Galleries	202 Aberdeen St	03 5223 1825
343 Gallery	Galleries	343 Packington St	03 5222 2157
Geelong Art Society Inc (Shearers Arms Gallery)	Galleries	202 Aberdeen Street	03 5223 1825
Geelong Gallery SEE AD ON PAGE 47	Galleries	Lt Malop Street	03 5229 3645
Leaf & Stone SEE AD ON PAGE 189	Galleries	51 McKillop St	03 5221 8083
Little Malop Gallery SEE AD ON PAGE 189	Galleries	101 Little Malop Street	03 5221 6505
Balyang Par 3 Golf Course	Golf Courses	Marnock Road	03 5222 3336
Barwon Valley Golf Club	Golf Courses	Barwon Heads Rd	03 5243 5443

Queens Park Public Golf Course	Golf Courses	Queens Park Road	03 5221 3592
Barking Dog Wine Bar & Café	Hotels	126 Pakington St	03 5229 2889
Belmont Hotel	Hotels	77 High St	03 5243 2802
Bush Inn	Hotels	58 Corio St	03 5229 5194
The Cremorne Hotel	Hotels	336 Pakington St	03 5221 2702
Icon Hotel	Hotels	69 Yarra St	03 5229 2922
Eureka Sportz Saloon Café	Hotels	98 Lt Malop St	03 5229 5266
Lord of the Isles Tavern	Hotels	3 West Fyans Street	03 5224 2522
Sawyers Arms Tavern	Hotels	2 Noble St	03 5223 1244
Scottish Chiefs Brewery	Hotels	99 Corio St	03 5223 1736
Wool Exchange Hotel	Hotels	59 Moorabool Street	03 5229 5577
Ford Discovery Centre SEE AD ON PAGE 189	Museum	Cnr Gheringhap & Brougham Sts	03 5227 8700
Leaf & Stone Garden Gallery	Nurseries	"Wintergarden, 51 McKillop St"	03 5222 8083
The Newtown Provedore	Provedores	317a Pakington St	03 5221 5654
V&R Fruit & Vegetable Market	Provedores	5 Pakington St	03 5222 2522
Warren & Hutch Provedores	Provedores	156 Pakington St	03 5229 7720
Barwon Booksellers SEE AD ON PAGE 189	Retail	2 James St	03 5221 8388
Bay City Newsagency	Retail	Shop 120 Bay City Plaza	03 5229 8201
Bell Park Newsagency	Retail	21 Milton St	03 5278 4032
Bellarine Village	Retail	Bellarine Hwy	03 9275 7777
Belmont Authorised Newsagency	Retail	132a High St	03 5243 1385
Books Around	Retail	137b Pakington St	03 5224 2150
Bunches & Buds Florist & Gifts & Café	Retail	48 Watsons Rd	03 5248 6199
Collins Booksellers Pty Ltd	Retail	96 Ryrie St	03 5221 6811
Corio Village Newsagency	Retail	19 Labuan Sq	03 5277 3034
Corio Village Newsagency	Retail	Corio Village Centre	03 5275 1666
Corio Village Newsagency	Retail	Shop 27 Bacchus Marsh Rd	03 5275 6829
Dymocks Booksellers	Retail	Market Square Shopping Centre Plaza	03 5229 5755
East Geelong Newsagency	Retail	78a Garden St	03 5229 5109
Garden Street Books	Retail	168 Yarra St	03 5229 1667
Geelong & Bellarine Books	Retail	72 Garden St	03 5229 2170
Geelong Authorised Newsagency & Lotto Pty Ltd	Retail	Shop 12/ Market Sq	03 5221 9094
Geelong Authorised Newsagency & Lotto Pty Ltd	Retail	Shop 12/ 140 Malop St	03 5221 9095
Geelong North Newsagency	Retail	185 Melbourne Rd	03 5278 2466
Geelong West Newsagency	Retail	198 Pakington St	03 5229 1973

Griffiths Bookstore	Retail	96 Ryrie St	03 5221 6811
Grovedale Newsagency Lotto and Post Office	Retail	19 Peter St	03 5243 1480
Highton Newsagency	Retail	7 Bellevue Ave	03 5243 4824
Imageworks	Retail	100 Fyans St	03 5229 6222
Just Because on Barrabool	Retail	"Shop 3, 65-71 Barrabool Rd"	03 5244 2800
Juswool Pty Ltd (subsidiary of Hedrena P/L)	Retail	10-14 Eastern Beach	03 5221 2650
Keswick Bookshop Inc.	Retail	364 Pakington St	03 5222 2228
Manifold Newsagency	Retail	132 Shannon Ave	03 5229 5897
Market Square Shopping Centre	Retail	Malop St	03 5221 2411
Prestige - Jayco Geelong	Retail	182-192 Bellarine Hwy	03 5248 6655
"R & B Smith, Holden"	Retail	510 Moorabool Street	03 5222 2888
Rays Outdoors	Retail	340 Melbourne Road	03 5278 7633
Resistance Books	Retail	68 Little Ryrie St	03 5222 6900
Tasman Gallery - Tasmanian Blackwood Furniture	Retail	3 Melbourne Rd	03 5278 6558
Westfield Bay City	Retail	"Centre Management, Malop St"	03 5221 4966
Wintergarden	Retail	51 McKillop St	
Jens Gaunt SEE AD ON PAGE 187	Service	Geelong	03 5222 1333
Geelong Harness Racing Club	Sports Club	"Beckley ParkPrinces Hwy"	03 5275 4880
Geelong Racing Club	Sports Club	Breakwater Road	03 5229 4414
Royal Geelong Yacht Club Inc	Sports Club	Eastern Beach	03 5229 3705
The Rock Adventure Centre	Sports Club	"River End, Rear 403Pakington St"	03 5221 3101
Gull Airport Service	Tourism Services	45 McKillop Street	03 5222 4966
Pack & Send Geelong	Tourism Services	6 Mercer St	03 5221 8411
Travelex Australasia Pty Ltd	Tourism Services	"Shop 2, 102 Moorabool Street"	03 5223 2666
Weddings with Oomph	Tourism Services	"The Olde Dairy, 111 Hope St"	03 5229 6556
Cross Country Express Pty Ltd	Tours and Transport	60 Rose Ave	03 5274 1009
Freedom Bay Cruises	Tours and Transport	1-11 Eastern Beach	0418 522 328
Gallivantours	Tours and Transport	244 Roslyn Rd	03 5244 0908
Geelong Tour Guiding	Tours and Transport	8 Norfolk Ave	03 5241 1769
Icon Tours	Tours and Transport	6 Moreton Bay Drive	0425 735 994
Southern Cross Motorcycle Tours	Tours and Transport	10 Dundas Street	03 5222 4361
Tarts 'N' Tyrants	Tours and Transport	1/42 Sanglen Terrace	03 5243 9391
Thrifty Car Rental	Tours and Transport	15 York St	03 5222 5888
Austin's Barrabool Winery	Wineries	50 Lemins Road	03 5241 8114
Pettavel Pty Ltd	Wineries	65 Pettavel Rd	03 5266 1120

■	Prince Albert Vineyard	Wineries	100 Lemins Road	03 5241 8091
■	Waybourne Winery	Wineries	60 Lemins Road	03 5241 8477
■	Wine Geelong	Wineries	PO Box 353	03 5254 1248
LARA				
■	Lara's Bed & Breakfast Penny Royal	Accommodation	25 West Gateway	03 5282 2813
■	Short Getaway	Accommodation	300 Patullos Rd	0421 022 230
■	Serendip Sanctuary	Eco Tourism	100 Windermere Road	03 5282 1584
■	Elcho Park Golf Course	Golf Courses	Elcho Road	03 5282 1582
■	Roraima Nursery	Nurseries	20 Swan Street	03 5282 8704
■	Lara Newsagency	Retail	44 The Centreway	03 5282 1419
■	Avalon Airport	Tourism Services	Beach Road	03 5227 9100
LEOPOLD				
■	Carville Retreat	Accommodation	2 Hannan Crescent	03 5250 5479
■	Pelican Shores - Geelong BIG 4 Holiday Park	Accommodation	300 Clifton Ave	03 5250 1382
■	Pelican Shores - Geelong BIG 4 Holiday Park	Accommodation	300 Clifton Ave	03 5250 1382
■	Toorang Lakeside Retreat	Accommodation	405 Melaluka Rd	03 5250 4609
■	Leopold Sportsmans Club Inc	Entertainment Centre	135 Kensington Rd	03 5250 2250
■	Leopold Newsagency & Tattslotto	Retail	45 Ash Rd	03 5250 1687
LETHBRIDGE				
■	Moranghurk	Accommodation	Midland Highway	03 5331 4334
■	Amietta Vineyard & Winery	Wineries	30 Steddy Road	03 5281 7407
LITTLE RIVER				
■	Little River Earth Sanctuary	Eco Tourism	985 Little River - Ripley Rd	03 5283 1602
MARCUS HILL				
■	Bellarine Park	Accommodation	1770 Bellarine Hwy	03 5256 1963
MOOLAP				
■	Moolap Caravan Park	Accommodation	365 Bellarine Highway	03 5250 1381
■	Moolap Caravan Park (BPT)	Accommodation	365 Bellarine Highway	03 5250 1381
■	Out West Miniature Farm	Attractions	115 Moolap Station Road	03 5248 2173
MOORABOOL				
■	Jindalee Estate Pty Ltd	Wineries	265 Ballan Road	03 5276 1280
MT DUNEED				
■	Bennickim Gallery	Galleries	215 Whites Rd	0438 818 025
OCEAN GROVE				
■	16 Mermaid	Accommodation	16 Mermaid Ave	03 5255 5843

Bellarine Cottage	Accommodation	50 Ocean Grand Drive	03 5255 5245
Boat Ramp Motel	Accommodation	14-18 Guthridge Street	03 5255 2018
Collendina Caravan Park	Accommodation	177 Bonnyvale Road	03 5255 1966
Green Valley Caravan Park	Accommodation	14 The Terrace	03 5255 1605
King Tide Townhouse	Accommodation	"UNIT 6, 12-14 Sweetman Pde"	03 5254 1571
Lavender Cottage by the Sea	Accommodation	27 Orton St	03 5256 3648
Ocean Grove Gardens Motel	Accommodation	17-19 Lake Ave	03 5256 1199
Ocean Grove Holiday Park	Accommodation	90 Wallington Road	03 5256 2233
Ocean Grove Motor Inn	Accommodation	64-78 Wallington Road	03 5256 2555
Ocean Grove Tower House	Accommodation	21 Trevally Dve	07 5447 2259
Ocean Hideaway	Accommodation	12 Woodlands Dve	03 5255 2192
Ocean House Bed & Breakfast	Accommodation	86 Presidents Ave	04 0917 6301
Ocean Sands Ocean Grove	Accommodation	27 Finch Close	03 5256 1616
Rathlin by the Sea	Accommodation	120 Dare St	0417 551 583
River Change House	Accommodation	13 Peers Cres	03 5256 2201
Riverview Family Caravan Park	Accommodation	Sweetman Pde	03 5256 1600
Seachange Villa on Dare	Accommodation	5/105 Dare Street	03 5256 3648
Surf Serenade	Accommodation	134 Orton St	03 5256 2397
The Terrace Lofts	Accommodation	92 The Terrace	03 5255 4167
Ti-Tree Village	Accommodation	34 Orton Street	03 5255 4433
Watermark	Accommodation	8 Inskip St	03 5255 1730
Wayawa Farm B&B	Accommodation	1070 Bellarine Hwy	03 5250 4457
Wynndean Holiday Resort	Accommodation	15 The Esplanade	03 5255 1766
KYO Pty Ltd	Antiques	26 Smithton Grove	03 5255 2444
Oakdene	Dining	255 Grubb Rd	03 5255 1255
The Mex	Dining	4 Grubb Road	03 5255 1959
Ocean Grove Hardware	Retail	81 The Terrace	03 5255 1201
Ocean Grove Newsagency	Retail	82 The Terrace	03 5256 1779
Ocean Grove Bowling Club	Sports Club	18 The Terrace	03 5255 1540
Kayak Connextions	Sports Club	154 Asbury Street East	03 5256 1679
Hendry Cycles-Oceanride	Sports Club	The Parade	03 5255 1627
POINT LONSDALE			
Akuna	Accommodation	18 Albert St	0418 334 978
Beach House - Point Lonsdale	Accommodation	36 Buckleys Rd	0407 866 568
Gull House	Accommodation	724a Shell Rd	0438 016 769

■	Longueville	Accommodation	25 Gill Road	03 5258 2990
■	Lonsdale Lakes Bed & Breakfast	Accommodation	60 Santa Monica Blvd	03 5258 3908
■	Lonsdale Light Houses	Accommodation	1 A Murray Road	03 5258 4860
■	Lonsdale Villas	Accommodation	87-93 Bellarine Hwy	03 5258 4533
■	Point Lonsdale Guesthouse	Accommodation	31 Point Lonsdale Road	03 5258 1142
■	Seahaven - Point Lonsdale	Accommodation	Unit 4 75 Point Lonsdale Rd	03 5258 1811
■	Springhill Retreat	Accommodation	10 Springhill Court	03 9376 2357
■	Queenscliffe Lighthouse Theatre Group Inc	Entertainment Centre	14 Hillcrest Dve	03 5258 3891
■	Muse Studio	Galleries	239 Pt.Lonsdale Rd	03 5258 1155
■	Nature's View Home Gallery	Galleries	35 Ward Rd	03 5258 3933
■	Lonsdale Golf Club	Golf Courses	69 Fellows Road	03 5258 1955
■	Point Lonsdale Newsagency	Retail	99 Point Lonsdale Rd	03 5258 1159
■	Bass Strait Fishing Charters	Sports Club	226 Fellows Road	03 5258 3067
■	Kyena Fishing Charter	Tours and Transport	4 Grimes Rd	03 5258 1424
PORTARLINGTON				
■	Arlingtons on Newcombe	Accommodation	132 Newcombe St	03 5259 3799
■	Bay Cottage at Portarlington	Accommodation	143 The Esplanade	03 9645 4081
■	Carrick	Accommodation	C/- Stockdale & Leggo	03 9534 9749
■	Dylene Caravan Park	Accommodation	5 Mercer Street	03 5259 2873
■	Foott Loose - Beach House	Accommodation	9 Simson St	03 5259 2248
■	Portarlington Beach Motel	Accommodation	153 Newcombe Street	03 5259 3801
■	Portarlington Holiday Units and Pool	Accommodation	84 Smythe St	03 5259 2910
■	Portarlington Seaside Resort	Accommodation	Sproat St	03 5259 2764
■	The Grand Hotel Portarlington	Accommodation	76 Newcombe St	03 5259 2260
■	The ol'Duke	Accommodation	40 Newcombe St	03 5259 1250
■	Waterview Bed & Breakfast	Accommodation	43 Clarke St	03 5259 1400
■	Portarlington Mill	Attractions	Turner Crt	03 5259 3847
■	The Grand Hotel Portarlington	Dining	76 Newcombe St	03 5259 2260
■	Gallery Estitique	Galleries	2 Brown St	0414 291 833
■	Portarlington Golf Club	Golf Courses	130 Hood Road	03 5259 2492
■	Portarlington Newsagency	Retail	Shop 1/ 60 Newcombe St	03 5259 2892
QUEENSCLIFF				
■	10 Osprey Mews	Accommodation	"Unit 10 Osprey Mews21-23 Hesse Street"	03 5258 3633
■	Athelstane	Accommodation	4 Hobson Street	03 5258 1024
■	"Banks, at Queenscliffe Bed & Breakfast"	Accommodation	78a Hesse Street	03 5258 4326

Benambra Bed & Breakfast	Accommodation	15 Hesse St	03 5258 2606
Big 4 Beacon Resort Holiday Park & Motel	Accommodation	78 Bellarine Highway	03 5258 1133
Boatramp Cottage	Accommodation	12 Bridge St	03 5258 4662
Bridie's	Accommodation	7 Mason Court	03 8623 5338
Brigadoon	Accommodation	40 Mercer St	03 5258 3343
Glenkelso Holiday Apartments	Accommodation	21-23 Hesse St	03 5258 1606
Historic Gordon Terrace 1890	Accommodation	36 Stokes St	03 5231 5335
Kent House B & B	Accommodation	15 Swanston Street	03 5258 3501
Lathamstowe Guest House	Accommodation	44 Gellibrand St	03 5258 4110
Maytone By The Sea	Accommodation	68 Stevens Street	03 5258 4059
Ozone Hotel SEE AD ON PAGE 165 & 189	Accommodation	42 Gellibrand Street	03 5258 1011
Queenscliff Hotel	Accommodation	16 Gellibrand Street	03 5258 1066
Queenscliff Inn	Accommodation	59 Hesse Street	03 5258 4600
Queenscliff Lavender Farm	Accommodation	6 McDonald Rd	03 5258 3389
Queenscliff Sea Side Cottages	Accommodation	96 Hesse Street	0414 520 248
Queenscliff Tourist Parks	Accommodation	138 Hesse St	03 5258 1765
Riptide Motel & Holiday Units	Accommodation	31 Flinders Street	03 5258 1675
Ruby's B&B	Accommodation	2 St Andrews Street	03 5258 4838
Seaview Guest House	Accommodation	86 Hesse Street	03 5258 1763
Springhill	Accommodation	13 Pardalote Close	03 5258 1446
The Pilot's House Bed & Breakfast	Accommodation	50 Gellibrand St	03 5258 4171
The Salt House	Accommodation	8 Wharf Street	0419 355 796
Twomey's Cottage	Accommodation	13 St Andrews Street	03 5258 1719
Vue Grand	Accommodation	46 Hesse Street	03 5258 1544
Waratah at Queenscliffe	Accommodation	104 Hesse Street	03 5258 3343
Wyuna Motor Inn	Accommodation	32 Hesse St	03 5258 4540
Bellarine Peninsula Railway	Attractions	Symonds Street	03 5258 2069
Fort Queenscliff Museum Inc	Attractions	King Street	03 5258 1488
Queenscliff Maritime Museum	Attractions	Weeroona Pde	03 5258 3440
Geelong & Bellarine Mopeds	Car Hire	PO Box 14	03 5258 4796
Vue Grand	Conference Centre	48 Hesse St	03 5258 3225
Ozone Hotel	Conference Centre	42 Gellibrand Street	03 5258 1011
Suma Park Conference Centre	Conference Centre	2135 Bellarine Hwy	03 5258 3507
Sails Restaurant	Conference Centre	32 Hesse St	03 5258 4540
Athelstane	Dining	4 Hobson Street	03 5258 1024

Queenscliff Hotel	Dining	16 Gellibrand Street	03 5258 1066
Royal Hotel Queenscliff	Dining	34 - 38 King Street	03 5258 1669
Seaview Guest House	Dining	86 Hesse Street	03 5258 1763
Vue Grand	Dining	46 Hesse Street	03 5258 1544
Marine Discovery Centre	Eco Tourism	Weeroona Pde	03 5258 3344
Queenscliff Music Festival Inc.	Entertainment Centre	PO Box 148	03 5258 4816
Queens Gallery	Galleries	65 Hesse St	03 5258 4388
Russell Davis	Galleries	15 Mercer St	03 5258 3156
Seaview Gallery	Galleries	86 Hesse Street	03 5258 3645
Queenscliff Golf Club	Golf Courses	Swan Island	03 5258 1951
Queenscliffe Historical Museum Inc SEE AD ON PAGE 189	Museum	49 Hesse St	03 5258 2511
Animal Instincts	Retail	69 Hesse St	03 5258 4226
at coastal road - home	Retail	54 Hesse St	03 5258 2709
"Tinnpott, Quagfire & Hagg"	Retail	70 Hesse St	03 5258 3973
Eddies on Mainstreet	Retail	66 Hesse St	03 5258 3944
Barwon Booksellers Pty Ltd SEE AD ON PAGE 189	Retail	81 Hesse St	03 5221 8388
Queenscliff Newsagency	Retail	72 Hesse St	03 5258 1828
Queenscliff Presence	Retail	2 Hobson Street	03 5258 3399
The Bookshop at Queenscliff	Retail	4/44 Hesse St	03 5258 2422
The Tenby Store	Retail	Cnr Hesse & Hobson Sts	03 5258 2098
Jens Gaunt SEE AD ON PAGE 187	Service	Queenscliff	03 5258 3633
Queenscliff Dive Centre	Sports Club	37 Learmonth St	1800 814 200
"Queenscliff Bowling, Tennis & Croquet Club"	Sports Club	118 Hesse St	03 5258 1773
Bellarine Peninsula Railway	Tours and Transport	Symonds Street	03 5258 2069
Game and Recreational Fishing Charters	Tours and Transport	PO Box 113	03 5258 2802
Impulse Charters Queenscliff	Tours and Transport	Queenscliff	03 5258 3739
Peninsula Searoad Transport Pty Ltd	Tours and Transport	Larkin Pde	03 5258 3244
Queenscliff Historical Tours & Bike Hire	Tours and Transport	72 Nelson Road	03 5258 3403
Ruby's Marine Charters	Tours and Transport	2 St Andrew St	03 5258 4838
Sea All Dolphin Swims	Tours and Transport	Queenscliff Boat Habour	03 5258 3889
RYE			
Netbookings	Tourism Web Service	9 Louise Street	03 5985 9015
ST LEONARDS			
Bellarine Rose Cottage B&B	Accommodation	272 Harvey Road	03 5241 1683
Edwards Point Beach Villas	Accommodation	7 Ord Street	03 5253 3461

■	St Leonards Caravan Park	Accommodation	99 Leviens Road	03 5257 1490
■	St Leonards-by-the-bay-Pelican's Rest	Accommodation	2/22 Bell Parade	03 5257 3429
■	St Leonards Newsagency & General Store	Retail	1383 Murradoc Rd	03 5257 1433
SWAN BAY				
■	Swan Bay Boat Hire	Tours and Transport	1195 Queenscliff Rd	03 5258 1780
TORQUAY				
■	Pear Tree Products	Retail	"Shop 7, 7 Gilbert St"	03 5261 6375
■	Torquay Books	Retail	Shp1B/ 9 Gilbert St	03 5261 2311
■	Torquay Christian Bookshop	Retail	20 Pearl St	03 5261 4214
■	Torquay Newsagency	Retail	20 Gilbert St	03 5261 2448
■	Jens Gaunt SEE AD ON PAGE 187	Service	Torquay	03 5261 4001
WALLINGTON				
■	Moke Manor	Accommodation	325 Swan Bay Rd	03 5251 3398
■	Wallington Roseglen	Accommodation	1180 Bellarine Highway	03 5250 1709
■	All Aboard Old Wares and Collectables	Antiques	1610 Bellarine Hwy	03 5250 1072
■	Adventure Park	Attractions	5 Swan Bay Road	03 5250 2756
■	Bellarine Adventure Golf	Attractions	Cnr Bellarine Highway & Grubb Road	03 5250 3777
■	Barwon Buses (Bellarine Food & Wine Tours)	Tours and Transport	128 Rhinds Road	03 5250 3930
WERRIBEE				
■	The Mansion Hotel at Werribee Park	Accommodation	K Road	03 9650 6386
■	The Mansion at Werribee Park	Attractions	K Road	03 9741 2444
■	Victoria's Open Range Zoo at Werribee	Attractions	K Road	03 9731 9632
■	The Mansion Hotel at Werribee Park	Conference Centre	K Road	03 9731 4000
■	The Mansion Hotel at Werribee Park	Dining	K Road	03 9731 4000
■	National Celtic Folk Festival	Entertainment Centre		

COLOUR KEY

Accommodation	Antiques	Association
Car Hire	Care Rental	Conference
Dining	Eco Tourism	Eductaion
Entertainment	Event Group	Galleries
Golf Courses	Hotel	Museums
Nurseries	Provedure	Retail
Services	Sport	Tourism Services
Tours and Transport	Web Services	Winereis

2 FACES THE RESTAURANT

An adventure in new taste sensations… Experience award winning contemporary fine dining in 1857 heritage surroundings. Friendly service, relaxed ambience & fully licensed. Recommended by The Age Good Food Guide.

8 Malop St. Geelong 3220
T: [03] 5229 4546
www.geelonginfo.com/2faces

BARWON BOOKSELLERS

The largest secondhand bookseller in country Victoria. Buying and selling quality secondhand books.

2 James St. Geelong
T: [03] 5221 8388

81 Hesse St. Queenscliff
T: [03] 5258 4522

BELLBRAE ESTATE – LONGBOARD WINES

Situated close to Bells Beach, at 520 Great Ocean Road Bellbrae, Longboard wines are a direct reflection of the cool maritime climate and relaxed coastal lifestyle.

Cellar Door and Café: open 11.00 am to 5.00 pm
Winter – Sat. & Sun. and Public Hol. only
Summer – 1 Nov. to Easter, fri. to Mon. **January** – 7 Days
T: [03] 52648480
E: info@bellbraeestate.com.au
www.bellbraeestate.com.au

BELLBRAE HARVEST

Restaurant Produce Accommodation
A delightful country property 15 mins from Torquay & Angelsea offering a fine array of creature comforts. Here you will discover a charming mudbrick restaurant & 3 boutique accommodation units. Enjoy the beauty.

45 Portreath Road Bellbrae 3228
T/F: (03)5266 2100
www.bellbraeharvest.com.au

EMPIRE GRILL

Whether it's an intimate dinner or a corporate occasion the Empire Grill Restaurant has the ultimate dining experience. Private dining & function rooms available. Comfortable surroundings & friendly staff.

66 Mckillop Street Geelong 3220
T: [03] 52232132
E: dine@empiregrill.com.au
www.empiregrill.com.au

FORD DISCOVERY CENTRE

The Ford Discovery Centre is Australia's first interactive museum that provides a behind the scenes opportunity to experience how cars are designed, engineered and built … take the journey through the Australian history of Ford.

Cnr Gheringhap & Brougham Sts Geelong 3220
T: [03] 5227 8700 **F:** [03] 7227 8707
www.forddiscovery.com.au

LEAF & STONE

Original Artworks for gardens displayed in a Courtyard Garden setting. Visit our historic 1854 building housing boutique shops and enjoy breakfast, lunch or coffee in the Cafe' Bar…. at the Wintergarden

51 McKillop St. Geelong
T: [03] 5221 8083
www.leafandstone.com.au

LITTLE MALOP GALLERY

Fine contemporary art in Geelong's Arts & Cafe Precinct. Diverse and exciting list of artists represented. We provide the opportunity and advice to acquire quality artworks for enjoyment and investment.

101 Little Malop Street Geelong 3220
(behind Flight Centre) **T:** [03] 5221 6505
www.littlemalopgallery.com.au

MT ANAKIE WINERY

Situated in a lovely valley, set in a rustic Austrian style atmosphere, with red deer looking in at you through the window. Cellar door open 7 days a week 11am-5pm. Functions catered for 20-80 people. Bookings essential.

130 Staughton Vale Rd. Anakie 3221
T: [03] 5284 1256 **F:** [03] 5284 1405

NARANA CREATIONS

Aboriginal art and crafts – paintings, and didgeridoos. A varied cultural programme enables groups to participate in a variety of activities including an exploration of the native garden and its foods. Free entry 9am-5pm, Mon to Fri; 10am-4pm, Sat

410 Torquay Rd, Grovedale
T: [03] 5241 5700 **E:** info@narana.com.au
www.narana.com.au

OZONE HOTEL

With Victorian decore in all rooms and a favourite with holiday makers for over a century, the hotel has enjoyed many awards and achievements and is recommended by the Age Good Food Guide.

42 Gellibrand Street Queenscliff 3225
Tel: [03] 5258 1011 **Fax:** [03] 5258 3712
Email: info@ozonehotel.com.au
www.ozonehotel.com.au

QUEENSCLIFFE HISTORICAL MUSEUM INC.

Memories of Queenscliff and Point Lonsdale can be reignited through the many objects of interest including art, photographs, documents and clothing on display daily at the Queenscliffe Historical Museum.

49 Hesse St (or PO Box 135) Queenscliff 3225
T: [03] 5258 2511
E: qhminfo@pipeline.com.au

PHOTOGRAPHY CREDITS

Best Shot! aims to reveal the landscapes locals know – and often take for granted - in ways that sometimes startle, but always capture the 'spirit of place'.

Best Shot! books, calendars, and cards are vehicles for the photographic visions of local artists who are passionate about their home territory.

A diverse and talented group of nine photographers has contributed to the Geelong & the Bellarine Peninsula book. Each brings a unique perspective to the region, and each has the gift of showing the viewer new ways to see the world.

Many of the photographs in this book are available framed. If you would like a framed version of any photograph, see www.bestshot.com.au for more information, or contact Best Shot! for details on a range of prices and sizes (email click@bestshot.com.au. or freecall 1300 66 49 43).

Best Shot! is always on the lookout for new and atmospheric photographs, and welcomes submissions from anyone – young or old, professional or amateur - who has captured an aspect of Geelong & the Bellarine Peninsula and who would like to share their image with the world.
See www.bestshot.com.au for more details.

ROBYN ALSOP

A loving partner of 19 years, seven beautiful children and a desire to change her life after depression led Robyn to a career in photography. Partnered with her daughter Julia, their company Jolie Image has a vision to bring change to the fundraising family portraiture niche market. Robyn loves photography with all its myriad subjects and her desire to continually explore photography led to her current studies at Brougham Art School. Robyn attributes her success in life to the many valued friendships she maintains and her faith in God.

Contact Jolie Image, tel 0400 938 845

ROBERT BOLE

Robert Bole is an outdoor wilderness photographer who has traveled to many areas of Australia. Robert strongly believes in photographic integrity and never uses coloured filters or any digital intervention; all his photographs are taken with colour transparency film. Many of his images are taken in extremely low light, using very long exposures, and the results are extraordinary. Robert has recently exhibited in the Warrnambool Art Gallery, the Portland CEMA Arts Centre, and the Gordon Gallery. He is scheduled to exhibit at the Geelong Art Gallery in June 2005. Selected images hand printed to Ilford Cibachrome are available from Robert's website.

Contact Aussie Escapes, www.aussiescapes.com.

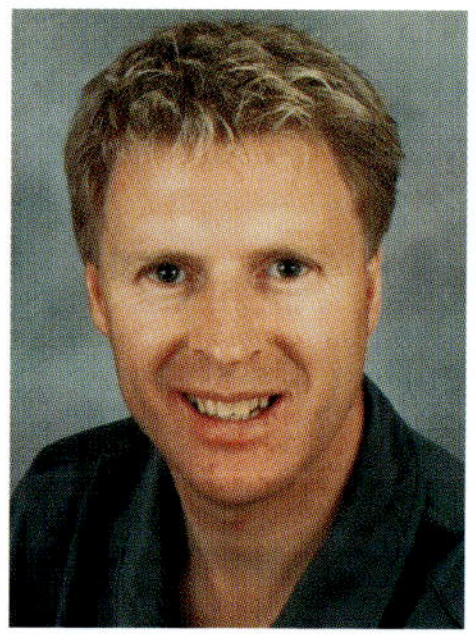

BARRY FELDMAN

Barry Feldman has been involved in photography for over 15 years and now works full time as a school, wedding and portrait photographer. He is passionate about photographing landscapes and seascapes and says, 'I love capturing forever a beautiful image that is immersed in natural, glorious light.'

Contact Barry Feldman, tel 0410 519 298

BRUCE KIRBY

Bruce Kirby is a self-taught freelance photographer, with a travel bug. He took up photography after a career as a nightclub DJ, MC and entertainer in Australia and overseas. His photographic work covers a wide range of people and businesses, including special effects stunts. He currently works for What's On in Geelong? magazine, photographing product and editorials, and the City of Greater Geelong (Environmental). He has an extensive archive of local photographs and of photographs taken on his travels.

Contact Natural Photographic Impressions, tel 0419 156 987

JOE MORTELLITI

Joe Mortelliti's passion for photography began when he was given a darkroom developing kit for his 13th birthday. He was hooked from the first time he saw images coming up in a developing tray.... These days Joe shoots on a digital camera, but he remains a purist and does not manipulate the images on computer. Joe and his wife Marion are working on a book of photographs covering Victoria and they are currently exploring the hidden corners of the state. Selected images printed on archival silver halide photographic paper are available on their website.

Contact Lifestyle Images of Australia,
www.images-australia.com.au

JUDY SCANLON

Judy Scanlon's passion is surf and scenic photography, and she specialises in Bells Beach, Winkipop and Anglesea. She began taking photographs in 1999 – pursuing her interest in surf and the outdoors. She loves chasing wave shots, and her favourite wave is Winkipop. She sells prints from home, and from various retail outlets in Torquay and Aireys Inlet.

Contact Surfangle Photography, tel 0412 560 317

NATALIE J. RUSSEL

Natalie J. Russell resides in Torquay and is currently undertaking study in a Bachelor of Visual Arts. Working as a freelance photographer as well as at a photographic studio, Natalie is keen to head overseas again with her camera. Natalie particularly enjoys capturing environmentally sensitive photographs as well as documentary and street photography - capturing the themes of intimacy and humour.

Contact Natalie Russel, njrphotography@yahoo.com

ARTIST PHOTOGRAPHER COMMERCIAL

The specialist in corporate photography, Geelong-based Artist Photographer Commercial has been helping companies around Australia and overseas for over 20 years. Their specialty is creating images that help clients to enhance their brand(s) and increase their profitability. The friendly team at Artist Photographer works in partnership with their client to ensure that great photography helps their client stand apart from the competition. With offices Australia-wide, in Asia and the USA, talented photographers are able to work on a local level or on a much broader scale.

Contact Artist Photographer on Freecall 1800 063888,
or visit www.artistphotographer.com/commercial

GEORGE STAWICKI

George Stawicki works with a variety of commercial, educational and industrial clients, but has a particularly strong interest in architectural and artistic subjects. He has taken portraits of many of Geelong's artists, writers and sculptors. His intuitive, sensitive portraits also feature in wedding photography. George specialises in aerial photography. He lectures in photography at the Gordon Institute of TAFE.

Contact My Photos, tel 5224 2202

BESTSHOT!

Best Shot! publishes books, calendars, posters and cards that celebrate the landscapes, buildings and people of regional Victoria. Best Shot! is for people who understand 'the spirit of place'.

- www.bestshot.com.au
- Coffee-table guidebooks
- Large 'art' calendars
- Regular calendars
- Cards and posters
- Framed photographs

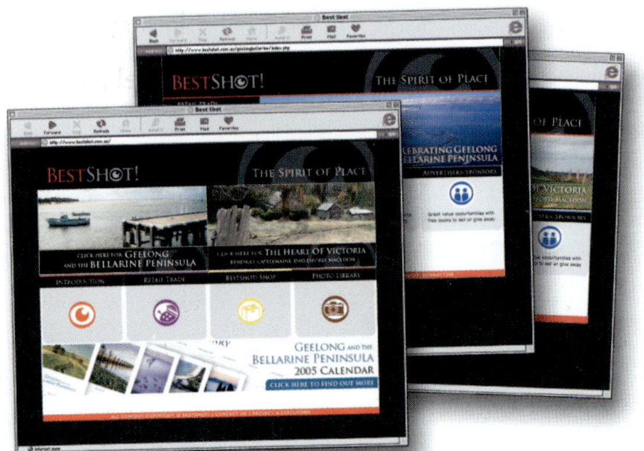

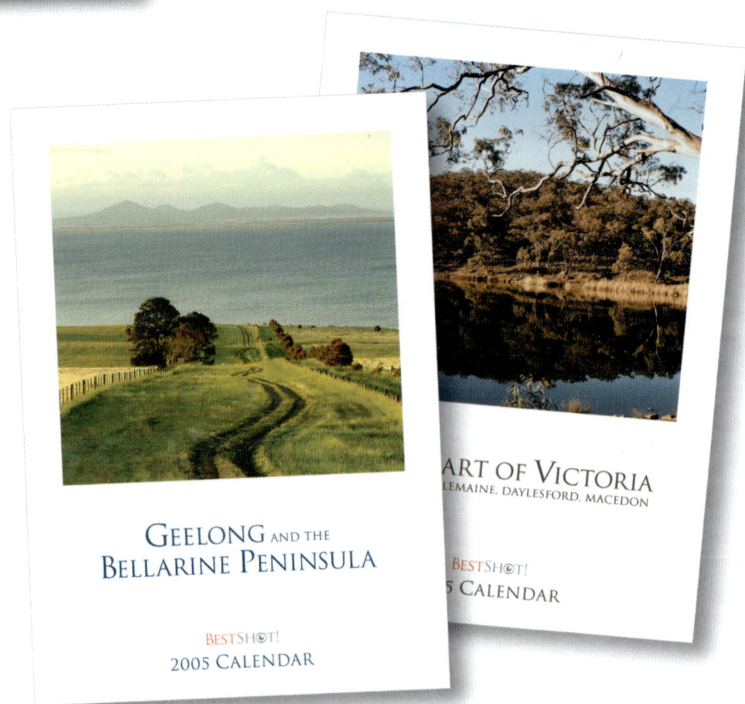

For more information:

See: www.bestshot.com.au
Email: click@bestshot.com.au
Freecall: 1300 66 49 43